D0824671

4/03

MODERN
NATIONS
—OF THE—
WORLD

HUNGARY

MODERN
NATIONS
—OF THE—
WORLD

HUNGARY

BY ANNE AKE

LUCENT
BOOKS ®

THOMSON

GALE

San Diego • Detroit • New York • San Francisco • Cleveland • New Haven, Conn. • Waterville, Maine • London • Munich

Thank you

*The author would like to thank Peter, Judit, and Imre Makrai
of Budapest for their warm hospitality and excellent information,
with a special thank you to Peter for serving as research assistant,
tour guide, and good friend. In the United States, longtime friends
Zoltan Bush, Vickie Bush, Lewis Bush, and Catherine Bush
provided insights into their beloved homeland, as well as historical information and manuscript assistance.*

© 2003 by Lucent Books. Lucent Books is an imprint of The Gale Group, Inc.,
a division of Thomson Learning, Inc.

Lucent Books® and Thomson Learning™ are trademarks used herein under license.

For more information, contact
Lucent Books
27500 Drake Rd.
Farmington Hills, MI 48331-3535
Or you can visit our Internet site at http://www.gale.com

LIBRARY OF CONGRESS CATALOGING-IN-PUBLICATION DATA

Ake, Anne, 1943–
    Hungary / by Anne Ake.
p.cm. — (Modern nations of the world)
Includes bibliographical references and index.
Summary: Discusses the diversity of Hungary and the struggle between the East and
West for control of it.
    ISBN 1-56006-970-8 (hardback : alk. paper)
  1. Hungary—Juvenile literature. [1. Hungary.] I. Title. II. Series.
    DB906 .A27 2002
    943.9—dc21

2001005699

CONTENTS

INTRODUCTION

WHERE EAST MEETS WEST

British poet Rudyard Kipling wrote, "Oh, East is East, and West is West and never the twain shall meet."[1] But East and West did meet and overlap more than a thousand years ago in the land of mountains and prairies that would eventually become Hungary. The mix has often been volatile.

The two great cultures—East (Asia) and West (Europe)—were isolated from each other for thousands of years. They developed very different philosophies, lifestyles, and religions. During the earliest centuries of recorded time, large groups of people in both the East and West migrated from place to place, following game, waterways, or the natural contours of the land. Gradually, these migrations closed the gap between the two cultures. In A.D. 896, a group of Eastern tribes called the Magyars (Hungarians) arrived in the fertile Carpathian basin in central Europe and a new nation was born. Historian C.A. Macartney wrote:

> No state in European history has a beginning so precisely definable as Hungary. It was brought into being . . . by a single act, when the Magyars, until then a people without fixed abode, entered the [Carpathian] basin . . . , and made it their home.[2]

The new Magyar nation was the farthest outpost of Eastern culture. Their nearest neighbors, the outermost fringe of Western culture, lived in permanent settlements to the north and west of the new Magyar home. Conflict between the two cultures was inevitable. The Magyars were aggressive people who sent raiding parties into the surrounding lands to steal from their western European neighbors. So began the power struggle that would shape the history of the area.

The Magyar lifestyle reflected that struggle for power as they learned new skills and customs from both their Eastern and Western neighbors. The Magyars adopted many elements and values of European society, including the Christ-

ian religion. A long history of domination by the Ottoman
Turks, however, brought renewed influences from the East.
Thus, the unique culture that developed in Hungary was distinct from both its European and Asian neighbors, while
gaining strength and resiliency from each.

The architecture, art, cuisine, and philosophy of Hungary
reflect the dual influences. Hungarian art and architecture,
for instance, have thrived on the broad range of cultural
blending. The Hungarians' love of coffee and tobacco can be
linked to the many years of Turkish occupation, and the fine
beers and wines produced in Hungary rival those of their
Western neighbors. The intellectual life of Hungary also reflects the dual influences. Hungary's universities are Western
in nature, but several are noted for their Asian studies pro-
grams. A scholarly paper published on the Internet traces the
growth of Asian studies in Hungary. Its author writes, "The
Orient [Asia] to our people represents more than just a geo-
graphical notion, since history proves that there are no other

countries, peoples or languages in Central Europe that are tied by so many bonds to the Orient as are the Hungarians."[3]

For hundreds of years Hungary's bonds to both European and Asian cultures served as the ropes in a tug-of-war between East and West, with Hungary caught in the middle. Even modern history reflects this struggle. For instance, the Hungarians, freed from the domination of Austria's Habsburgs after World War I, found themselves leaving World War II as citizens of a country controlled by the Soviet Union, an Eastern power.

Today, the new democratic Hungary seeks to reestablish strong ties to the West, but as an independent nation that cherishes its diverse heritage. In his book *The Spirit of Hungary*, Hungarian writer Stephen Sisa says:

> These new generations of Hungarians rooted in the West may help the Hungarian nation achieve her just aspirations and accomplish what a modern idol of their ancestral land, Béla Bartók [a Hungarian composer], expressed with these words: "We want to realize a synthesis of East and West. Our origins and geographic location has predestined us to such a role, for Hungary is at the same time the westernmost point of the East and a bastion of the West."[4]

A LAND OF GREAT DIVERSITY

In the late ninth century, the Magyar people made their way through the eastern European Carpathian Mountains into a sparsely inhabited land that invited them to stop and wander no more. The mountains dropped into a vast land of forest and prairie that stretched for hundreds of miles around the Danube and Tisza Rivers. The flat land was not ideal for growing crops because the rivers often overflowed their banks and flooded the surrounding plain. However, the floodwaters nurtured the native grasses, which provided prime grazing for cattle and horses. Farther west the flat land rose again into the foothills of the Austrian Alps. The gently rolling land between prairie and mountain was ideal for growing food crops and grapes for wines.

The land also provided an abundance of hot and cold water. The Danube, the Tisza, and several smaller rivers brought

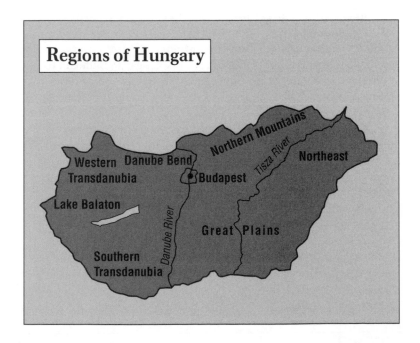

Regions of Hungary

Western Transdanubia
Danube Bend
Northern Mountains
Tisza River
Northeast
Budapest
Lake Balaton
Danube River
Great Plains
Southern Transdanubia

fresh, cold water from the mountains, and naturally hot water bubbled out of the ground from hundreds of thermal springs. In low places the plentiful water pooled to form more than a thousand lakes ranging in size from tiny ponds to the giant Lake Balaton—one of the largest in Europe.

MODERN HUNGARY

The land that the Magyars settled was vast, covering much of eastern and central Europe. Borders were redrawn from time to time, yet, until World War I, Hungary, as part of the Austro-Hungarian Empire, remained large and powerful. When the empire collapsed at the end of World War I, however, the Tri-

TAKING THE WATERS

Bathing in naturally warm spring waters is a tradition that dates back more than two thousand years in Hungary. The earth's crust is very thin in Hungary, so thermal waters rise easily to the surface. The result is approximately one thousand thermal springs scattered throughout the country. Baths ranging from simple community bathing places to elaborate spa complexes have been built around many of the springs. Some baths built during Turkish and Roman times are still in use.

Bathers from all over Europe flock to Hungary's thermal baths, not just for the relaxing warmth of the waters, but also for their healing powers. Because of their different mineral content, thermal waters from different springs are believed to benefit different ailments. Some relieve arthritis and other joint problems, while others are more beneficial for gastrointestinal ailments.

All together, Hungary's spa facilities can accommodate three hundred thousand bathers at the same time. Spas are located in twenty-two cities and sixty-two smaller towns. Budapest alone has approximately one hundred thermal springs providing waters for fifty baths. The most elaborate and best-known bath in Budapest is the Gellert bath at the Gellert Hotel. Its colorful tiles, marble columns, and stained-glass windows and ceilings provide a stunningly elegant setting for enjoying the healing waters. Outside of Budapest, one of the most spectacular spas is Lake Heviz, the largest thermal lake in Europe. The five-hundred acre lake is fed by a spring that pours out up to 80 million liters of warm water a day.

anon treaty of 1920 dealt harshly with Hungary for its involvement in the war. The treaty slashed away at Hungarian territory, leaving a small country approximately one-third of its prewar size. Hungary today covers only 35,911 square miles. It is about the size of the state of Indiana, and borders seven Eastern and Central European countries: Austria, Slovakia, Ukraine, Romania, Yugoslavia, Croatia, and Slovenia.

In spite of its reduced size, Hungary retains the topographical diversity that enticed the ancient Magyars to make their home there. The country includes mountains, plains, and rolling hills that divide it into three major geographic regions: the Northern Mountains, the Great Alfold (also called the Great Plain), and Transdanubia (the rolling hills and farmland west of the Danube River). These large, diverse areas can be subdivided into eight regions with similar geographic and cultural characteristics: Budapest, the Danube bend, Western Transdanubia, the Lake Balaton area, Southern Transdanubia, the Great Plain, the Northern Mountains, and the Northeast.

BUDAPEST

With nearly 2 million people, Budapest, Hungary's capital city, is home to 20 percent of the nation's population. It is a sophisticated, bustling city with an exciting blend of old and new, East and West, in its architecture and culture.

The current city of Budapest was created in 1873 when the smaller cities of Buda, Obuda, and Pest were combined, but its history goes back much further. In about the first century A.D., the warm waters, the strategic advantage of the region's high hills, and the rich hillside soil drew the Romans to the area around modern-day Budapest. They named their fortified camp Aquincum in honor of the thermal springs of the area and built elaborate baths around some of the springs. Some of the baths built by the Romans are still in use today. The Romans also grew grapes on the hillsides and established wine making as an important part of the economy of the region.

The Magyars arrived in the ninth century and built on the lowland that is now a fashionable section of Budapest, formerly the village of Obuda. Then, in the thirteenth century, King Bela IV, one of Hungary's most powerful kings, moved the political capital of the country to the city of Buda and built Buda Castle on a hill overlooking the Danube. Today,

LANGUAGE REVEALS HISTORY

The official language of Hungary is Hungarian (Magyar); it is spoken by 98 percent of the population of Hungary—about 10.5 million people. Hungarian is classified as part of the Finno-Ugric family of languages. Its closest relatives are the languages of Finland and Estonia. That does not mean that people speaking these languages can understand each other; only that linguists, people who study the origins and evolutions of languages, can show that the origins of these languages are the same. Linguists use similarities in language to trace the migration of people. The relationship between their languages suggests that many hundreds of years ago the Finnish, Estonian, and Magyar people originally came from the same part of Asia.

Hungarian's Asian origin has not been the only influence on the development of the language. As Hungarian has evolved, it has gained words from several other languages. Very early during their migrations, for example, the Magyar borrowed words from the Iranian and Turkic languages. More Turkish words were added during the long occupation of Hungary by the Turks. Then, due to years of living under Austrian rule, Hungarians adopted many German words. And thanks largely to American movies and music, some English words have been added to the language, especially by young people. Yet, in spite of the influences of these other languages, Hungarian remains unique. It is a beautiful and expressive language, and a source of pride to the Hungarian people.

Castle Hill houses the collection of the Hungarian National Gallery and the country's biggest library, the National Szechenyi Library.

Modern Budapest straddles the river, with the Buda side climbing up the green hills of the western bank. Castle Hill, restored after World War II, overlooks the river and offers a spectacular view of the capital. Across the Danube, the parliament building faces the river, and behind the building the busy cosmopolitan Pest section spreads over the flat plain. In the middle of the river lies one of the city's natural conservation areas, Margaret Island, almost two miles long and dotted with parks, sports grounds, swimming pools, and a spa hotel.

Eight bridges, all busy thoroughfares, span the Danube and connect the two sides of the city. The Chain Bridge, built in 1849, is flanked on each side by huge stone lions. It was the first bridge to be built across the river and is a favorite landmark for Budapest residents and visitors. In World War II, the Germans destroyed all of the Budapest bridges, so the existing bridges are reconstructions of the originals. All of the bridges were reconstructed in their original style with the exception of the Elizabeth Bridge, which was replaced with a new, modern bridge.

THE DANUBE BEND

Just north of Budapest, the Danube turns sharply south as it cuts between the Visegrad Mountains and the Borzsonyi Mountains. Castles and ancient cities sit atop cliffs and overlook the river below, making this bend of the river one of the most beautiful and historically significant areas of Hungary. The town of Esztergom, located near the northern end of the bend, was the medieval capital of Hungary and has been the Hungarian seat of Roman Catholicism for more than a thousand years.

Hungary's largest Roman Catholic cathedral sits above the Danube River in the town of Esztergom.

Other cities of the bend include Visegrad and Sentendre. Visegrad sits where the Romans built a border fortress during

the fourth century. In 1241, Hungary's King Bela built a castle on the river near the original Roman site and conducted much of the nation's business there. Thus, Visegrad was often called Hungary's other capital, and for several hundred years its scenery and cool mountain air made it popular with the Hungarian royal families during the summer months. A few miles away the ancient town of Sentendre, settled first by the Celts and later the Serbs, has become a thriving arts center. These historic cities and the beautiful scenery surrounding them draw thousands of tourists to the Danube bend each year.

WESTERN TRANSDANUBIA

The cultural and architectural influence of Hungary's four-hundred-year domination by the Habsburgs of Austria can be seen most clearly in the land west of the Danube bend. The Habsburgs left a distinctly Austrian mark on the area by building ornate Austrian-style castles near the existing medieval towns.

Austrians still seem to feel quite at home in Western Transdanubia and frequently cross the border into Hungary to vacation or shop. The landscape and architecture look much like Austria, and most of Western Transdanubia's inhabitants speak German—the language of Austria—as well as their native Hungarian. Austrians are also drawn across the border by lower Hungarian prices; stalls selling everything from dental services to household goods line roads near the border.

German-speaking tourists are not the area's only resource; Western Transdanubia is also one of the most industrialized parts of Hungary. The city of Gyor, the nation's third-largest industrial center, is best known for its production of trucks and textiles. In spite of its emphasis on heavy industry, Gyor's charming old-town section has many historically important buildings and monuments and is home to Hungary's most noteworthy ballet company, the Gyor Ballet Company.

A TOURIST MECCA

South and east of Western Transdanubia is Central Transdanubia, one of Hungary's most popular tourist areas. Two large lakes, Lake Balaton and Lake Heviz, dominate Central Transdanubia. Lake Balaton, with an area of 266 square miles, is one of Europe's largest lakes. Because the lake is very

shallow, its waters are warm enough for swimming early in the spring, when deeper lakes are still cold. Numerous resorts line the shores of the lake, which is popular with tourists from all over Hungary as well as neighboring countries. Nearby, Lake Heviz, with its floating garden of rare pink water lilies, is Europe's largest thermal spring-fed lake. Not only is it a comfortable place to swim even on the coldest winter day, but its warm mineral waters are believed to be beneficial in healing numerous health problems, ranging from arthritis to respiratory ailments.

Men play chess while relaxing in one of Hungary's many thermal lakes.

Although the economy of this area depends heavily on tourism, viticulture (growing grapes) is also important. Since the Middle Ages (the fifth to the fifteenth century) the Badacsony area on the north side of Lake Balaton has produced some of Hungary's finest wines.

SOUTHERN TRANSDANUBIA

The land south of the crowded Lake Balaton area is rural. In this area, called Southern Transdanubia, the land is relatively flat, although small mountain ranges such as the Mecsek Mountains protect it from the harsh northern winds. As a result, the climate here is milder and wetter than most of the country. There are some fairly large cities—Pecs, for example—but Southern Transdanubia is mainly an area of small villages. Agriculture is the backbone of the economy, with fruit orchards, almond groves, and vineyards spreading across the landscape.

Pecs is known for its varied architecture and its university. This region was the center of the one-hundred-and-fifty-year Turkish occupation, and some of the best-preserved examples of Turkish architecture in Hungary are in Pecs, including the Pasha Yakovali Hassan Mosque. Pecs has also been a university center since the Middle Ages, and today the University of Pecs is one of the finest in Hungary. In addition, Pecs also has a reputation as an art and cultural center, and people from all over the world visit its many galleries and museums. One noteworthy museum is the Csontvary Museum, which features the work of Kosztka Tivadar Csontvary (1853–1919), one of Hungary's greatest painters.

THE GREAT PLAIN

More than half of Hungary is flat. A huge prairie stretches south and east of Budapest, covering an area of twenty thousand square miles. The prairie extends from the foothills of the Carpathian Mountains in the north to the Romanian border to the east and to the southern border with Serbia. This is the Hungarian *puszta*, or plain. The *puszta* is best known for cattle and horse raising and the fine horsemanship of the *csikosok* (cowboys) who live there. Today, even though the economic importance of the livestock has diminished, the long-horned gray cattle and the *racka* sheep with their odd, twisted horns play a role in living-history exhibits, and the *csikosok* perform riding stunts for tourists.

Cowboys may be a trademark of the Great Plain, but agriculture is the mainstay of the area's economy, especially in the southern part of the plain. Thanks to modern irrigation, this part of the *puszta* is lush. Fields of corn, garlic, and peppers are broken by the brilliant yellow of acres of sunflowers. Sunflower seed oil, or sunseed oil as it is sometimes called, is an important Hungarian product for both domestic use and export.

Though mostly rural, the plain is dotted with several modern cities with ancient histories. Debrecen, with a population of 210,000, is Hungary's second-largest city. Since the Middle Ages, the city has had a reputation for wealth and conservative traditional values. The city's early wealth was based on salt, the fur trade, and cattle raising. Debrecen is also well known as the center of Protestantism in Hungary. Since the sixteenth century, many of Hungary's lawyers, doctors, and theologians have earned their degrees at Debrecen's Calvinist (Protestant) College.

With 177,000 people, Szeged, located on the Tisza River near the southern border with Yugoslavia and Romania, rivals Debrecen as the center of culture and education of the Great Plain. Szeged is known for its theater, opera, classical music performances, and its university.

Although Szeged has an ancient history dating back more than four thousand years, it has a more modern look than most Hungarian cities because almost all of Szeged's buildings were built during the late nineteenth century. The city

THE COWBOY TRADITION

A thousand years ago, Magyar warriors rode from the steppes of central Asia into the Carpathian basin, bringing with them a centuries-old tradition of fine horsemanship. Today, fine horsemanship is still a treasured tradition. In fact, many of Hungary's horse farms, including those owned by the state, have opened their doors to tourists and riding enthusiasts. They offer riding and carriage-driving excursions and lessons for all ages and skill levels.

Many of the riding farms also feature equestrian shows to demonstrate Hungarian riding skills. One of the most famous riding feats, the Puszta-five, is a recent innovation, but it has come to symbolize the romance of the *puszta* (Great Plain) and Hungarian horsemanship. In the Puszta-five, a Hungarian cowboy, or *csikos*, wearing traditional wide, white-linen trousers, controls five galloping horses, three in front and two behind. The *csikos* rides standing, with one foot on each of the two rear horses, and holds the reins of all five horses.

From stubby little ponies carrying ancient warriors to sleek powerful breeds such as the Nonius, horses have reflected the history and way of life of the Hungarians. Further, as working horses and as tourist attractions, they have always been a significant part of the country's folklore and economy.

was almost completely ruined in 1879 when the Tisza River flooded and destroyed 5,500 of the 5,800 houses in Szeged. In an international spirit of goodwill, cities from around the world, including Vienna, Paris, and London, contributed to the rebuilding of the city. To show their appreciation, the citizens of the reborn Szeged named many of their city streets after the foreign cities that helped rebuild the city.

NORTHERN HUNGARY

Hungary's highest peak is only about 3,300 feet, but the five ranges of mountains that make up northern Hungary are quite picturesque. The mountains are particularly popular with travelers seeking scenic vistas and the last traces of Old-World traditional lifestyles. In the Northern Mountains, more than anywhere else in Hungary, these traditions are well preserved.

Nestled among the vineyard-covered hills are several villages that seem to have escaped the passage of time. The Paloc and Matyo villagers are two Hungarian ethnic groups who, for hundreds of years, lived isolated lives in the hills and developed their own culture. They have clung to their traditional dress and way of life, and their villages are popular

A traditionally-dressed csikos *demonstrates his horsemanship in a riding feat known as the Puszta-five.*

gathering places for tourists who want to learn about the early life of the area. Old-style farming and cooking methods have been preserved, and traditional crafts such as needlework are still practiced. The Matyo people are noted for their colorful embroidery on a white or black background, and the Paloc are known for delicate white-on-white embroidery. In addition, the ancient city of Eger is popular with tourists who enjoy its history, charming old-town streets, and wineries.

Northern Hungary has one of the most varied landscapes in the nation. Hillsides covered by woods, deep dales, and sloping hills under agricultural cultivation alternate over the 6,600-square-mile area. Besides attracting tourists with its museums, traditional villages, spas, and holiday resorts, the region produces and exports some of Hungary's best-known wines, including the rich red Eger Bikaver (Bull's Blood), and sweet golden Tokaj.

A small mountain range, the Bukk Mountains, separates Eger from the industrial city of Miskolc, Hungary's third-largest city. Miskolc was once a busy steel-making center; however, the collapse of heavy industry in the early 1990s left it at the center of a polluted valley, in an area characterized by declining population, unemployment, and closed factories. Still, despite its depressed economic condition, Miskolc has much to offer. It is a gateway to the Bukk Mountains, and the alleged healing powers of the thermal baths of nearby Miskolctapolca are supposed to be the most beneficial in Hungary.

THE NORTHEAST

Hungary's Northeast region consists of just one culturally and physically distinct county, Szabolcs-Szatmar-Bereg. Though small, this region borders Slovakia, Romania, and Ukraine. Before the nineteenth century, surrounding swamplands and the flooding Tisza River kept the area isolated. This isolation protected the northeast from the destruction of the sixteenth-century Turkish invasion and preserved its most significant architectural feature—its historical wooden churches. Although more accessible today than in the past, the region's out-of-the-way location has prevented the Northeast from reaping the benefits of development. However, that may be changing as foreign investors such as America's General Electric Corporation take an interest in the area.

The Northeast is Hungary's most rural section: dirt roads, horse-drawn hay wagons, and thatched roofs are common sights. Fertile soil and gently rolling hills have helped make this area primarily agricultural, with apples as a major crop. Small villages dot the countryside, and the largest city, Nyiregyhaza, has a population of only 114,000.

The Northeast is also Hungary's most culturally diverse section. Before World War II, most Hungarian Jews living outside of Budapest lived in this area, and today some Jewish people still live in the area. In addition, a large percentage of Hungary's Roma, or Gypsy, population also resides in the Northeast.

As varied as these geographic regions are, together they form the background of the Hungarian national culture. Ethnic Hungarians comprise more than 89.9 percent of the country's population, and they take pride in their history and cultural background.

The Magyars:
Tugged Between
East and West

The great Magyar chieftain, Arpad, arrived in the land that is now Hungary in 896, leading seven tribes totaling about four hundred thousand people. Hundreds of years of traveling through rugged mountains and harsh climates had toughened Arpad's people. They learned self-defense and aggression by competing with other tribes who claimed the lands where the Magyars traveled.

When they arrived in the Carpathian basin, the Magyars must have been a fearsome sight. Hungarian historian Istvan Lazar describes them. He believes they arrived mounted on

short-legged, shaggy, brawny horses sweating mud, . . . On their shoulders, reflex bows composed of layers of sheets of horn cemented together with glue rendered from fish, hide, and bone, strengthened with coils of stag's sinew, and their tips and grasps made of antlers. On their left side, bundles of iron-tipped arrows in quivers; on their right, oriental sabres with curved, single-edged blades. Their saddles are high and rise sharply in front and back. This saddle and the Avar-type stirrup [a stirrup designed by an Eastern nomadic tribe] make it possible for both hands to be free in battle with reins flying to tear along hurling a shower of arrows in an attack on their enemy or, half-turned on their horses, to do so backwards fleeing from a superior force or feigning flight deceptively. They have become one with their horses, . . . their horses, on pressure from their knees or on command, wheel, stop dead, and start off. Their hair braided into pigtails held together on the sides by brass disks, those of the chiefs by gold ones. At their waists, the many studs on their leather belts as well as the embossed [decorated with raised designs], . . . U-shaped

21

Arpad, the great Magyar chieftain, takes possession of the land that would become Hungary.

plates on leather satchels containing their smaller belongings flash in the sunlight. They are hardy, like the wolves on the plains. They are fond of splendor, like the potentates [rulers] of the East.[5]

For hundreds of years, the area had hosted nomadic peoples from both East and West, but when the Magyars arrived, it stood almost empty as a buffer between the cultures of Europe and Asia. In the face of sometimes overwhelming pressures from the two conflicting cultures, the Magyars have made their home in Hungary for more than a thousand years.

CHANGING LIFESTYLES

The transition from hard-riding, nomadic barbarians to stable ranchers and farmers was not immediate. For most of the first century after their arrival in Hungary, Magyar warriors raided settlements as far away as Spain, southern Italy, and northern Germany. Their spoils included both wealth and slaves; they particularly liked raiding monasteries for their rich stores of gold ornaments.

The decision to settle into a more peaceful lifestyle came suddenly in 955, following a resounding defeat at the German city of Augsburg by Holy Roman Emperor Otto I. The Holy Roman Empire was a political and military counterpart of the Christian Church and was headed by the Holy Roman Emperor, who wielded considerable political, military, and spiritual power in Europe. Therefore, following the defeat at Augsburg, Prince Geza, the Magyar leader and Arpad's great-grandson, converted to Christianity in order to change his former enemy into a strong ally.

The conversion to Christianity had a major impact on the future of the emerging Hungarian nation. It steered the Magyars away from their Eastern ancestry and toward a Western lifestyle. The Western leaning was made stronger when King Stephen, Geza's son, decided to adopt the Roman alphabet, which made the Magyars' written language compatible with Western European languages. The combination of the two events set the Magyars on a Western course in education, scholarship, religion, and philosophy.

ST. STEPHEN

Geza's conversion was for political reasons, though, and he did not give up his old religion entirely. According to Macartney, "He is said to have declared himself 'rich enough to

THE HOLY ROMAN EMPIRE

During the tenth century, the Magyar found themselves battling a powerful alliance rather than individual villages. The alliance, which existed from 962 to 1806, was called the Holy Roman Empire. It was a loose federation of small European states representing the Christian (later, the Roman Catholic) Church and standing for the unity of all Christians.

In theory, the Holy Roman Empire was a civil counterpart to the Church, but it was also meant to be a political organization with one leader, called the Holy Roman Emperor, who ruled over all existing states. It never really fulfilled either premise. The Church, led by the pope, saw the empire as a secular extension of itself dedicated to protecting the Church and spreading the Christian faith. The emperors, on the other hand, often saw it as the path to personal wealth and power. These different viewpoints caused frequent conflict between popes and emperors throughout the existence of the empire.

afford two Gods.'"[6] His son, Stephen, on the other hand, was brought up as a Christian and was a true believer in the Christian doctrine. However, like his father, Stephen was aware of the political advantages offered by the Christian Church.

Thus, after Geza's death, Stephen declared war on the old Magyar religion. He ordered that his non-Christian enemies and their wives, children, and horses be buried alive. He also killed religious chanters (traveling musicians who spread their religious beliefs through song), or deafened them by pouring lead in their ears.

Stephen's dedication to the Church was well rewarded. On Christmas Day in the year 1000, Prince Stephen was crowned Christian King Stephen I with a crown sent from Rome by the pope. This elevated the loosely organized nation of Hungary to the status of a kingdom of the Holy Roman Empire. Macartney explains the significance of the religious conversion and the elevation of Stephen's position to king:

> It is impossible to over-emphasize the importance of these ceremonies. By them both Stephen's own status and that of his people were transformed. The act of conversion changed the Hungarian people from an outlaw horde against whom a Christian Prince was not only free, but bound by duty, to take up arms, into a member of the Christian family of nations, and their prince into one of those rulers by the Grace of God whose legitimate rights his fellow-princes could not infringe without sin. The royal crown made its wearer a true sovereign [supreme ruler] . . . while the Apostolic [from the pope] insignia made the Hungarian church free of any other authority save [except] that of Rome alone—an enormous reinforcement of the country's real independence.[7]

Under the protection of the Church, Stephen firmly established his authority. With the military and spiritual power of the Church behind him, he could force his policies on the people. Still, he did not disturb the traditional class structure of his people more than he thought necessary. As a result, the majority of the people, including nobles, freemen (descendants in the male line of the original Magyars), and peasants remained loyal to Stephen.

Under Stephen's leadership, a powerful new nation began to grow. His influence was so great that in 1088, forty-five

In 2000 the coronation crown of King Stephen I was placed on display to celebrate the 1000th anniversary of the founding of Hungary.

years after his death, he was declared St. Stephen by the Church and became Hungary's patron saint. Macartney describes St. Stephen as, "the best-loved, most famous and perhaps the most important figure in Hungarian history."[8]

A DEVELOPING NATION

Under Stephen, the blend of Eastern and Western cultures that characterizes the nation today began to take shape. The king's association with the Holy Roman Empire led Hungary to become Westernized in its military tactics, crafts, and clothing. Even so, the Hungarians still clung to many of their Eastern traditions. For example, many prominent persons began to dress like Western knights; while others preferred to wear Eastern-style silk caftans decorated in furs.

After Stephen's death in 1038, despite some disputes over succession, Hungary continued to expand and to forge stronger ties to Europe and the Church. The Hungarians conquered and colonized Transylvania, a mountainous land just to the east, and occupied Slavonia, now a part of Croatia. In 1103, Croatia came under Hungarian rule. By the end of the twelfth century, Hungary's land area had almost doubled since the original Magyar occupation, and the population had risen to almost 2 million. Through these acquisitions, Hungary had become one of the leading powers of southeastern Europe.

Macartney attributes much of the success of the emerging nation to the succession of kings of the Arpad dynasty. He writes:

> It must be said that Hungary was, on the whole, lucky in its kings. Quarrelsome as they were, they were generally able. . . . Ladislas I, who, like Stephen, was canonized [declared a saint by the Christian Church] after his death, was the outstanding personality among them: a true paladin [hero] and gentle knight, a protector of his faith and his people, and of the poor and defenseless. Kalman, nicknamed "the bookman," was . . . an exceptionally shrewd and enlightened ruler. . . . Several other of the Arpads were men of ability and of endearing nature. Of them all, only Stephen II was almost entirely bad, and Andrew II, irremediably silly.[9]

This stable political system was based on the absolute authority of the king. The king could levy taxes, for example, and demand the services of the nobles in wartime. Such a powerful king enabled Hungary to repel outside invaders and prevent internal unrest. Thus, the country continued to prosper.

During the thirteenth century, though, this changed when King Andrew II raised taxes on the serfs. This indirectly affected the income of the lesser nobles, and they rebelled. In 1222, as a result of the rebellion, Andrew was forced to sign the Golden Bull, a document that radically limited the king's power and raised the status of the lesser nobles. The document gave the nobles the right to resist the king, and stated that they would be called together for annual national assemblies in order to participate in decision making about how the country would be run. By allowing the nobles a voice in the government and the right to resist policies they did not like, Andrew took the first step in limiting the authority of the king.

WANING MAGYAR CONTROL

As the power of the king waned, the Magyar people also became vulnerable to outside interference. During the early thirteenth century, Mongolian forces under the leadership of Genghis Khan arrived from Asia. When the new Hungarian king Bela IV called on the nobles to mobilize against the Mongols, few responded, and the Mongols defeated Bela's small army in 1241. The invaders continued through the country, destroying towns and villages and eventually killing half of the population. The remaining population and villages were scattered and often impoverished. Hungarian historian Laszlo Makkai describes the devastation of the Mongol invasion:

> Mongol depredations lasting nearly a year had produced devastation unparalleled in Europe for centuries. . . . Damages caused by sword and fire were followed by famine and epidemics. A contemporary chronicler noted that "the calamity of bitter starvation decimated the Hungarian people as effectively as the Tatars' [Mongols]

THE BULL'S BLOOD OF EGER

Bull's Blood, the full-bodied red wine produced in the city of Eger in northern Hungary, got its name from an ancient battle in which wine played a role in saving the city. In 1552, the castle of Eger was besieged by a horde of Turkish soldiers; various sources estimate the number at anywhere from twenty thousand to one hundred thousand invaders. Military leader Istvan Dobos and two thousand villagers, including women and children, defended the castle. The men fought valiantly, and the women poured hot soup and oil on any enemy who neared the walls. According to legend, the defenders fortified themselves with the red wine produced by the village farmers. The men's beards were soon stained red with wine, and a rumor spread among the Turks that the Hungarians were such formidable opponents because they were drinking the blood of bulls. The villagers ultimately saved the city from the Turks, and the red wine of Eger has been known as Bull's Blood ever since.

In modern times, Eger Castle and Bull's Blood still protect the city—but now from economic decline. The ruins of the picturesque castle and the rich red wine, along with some excellent thermal baths, draw visitors from all over Eastern and Central Europe. Further, Eger Bull's Blood is exported all over the world and is probably the best known of Hungary's wines.

heartless butchery.". . . In the plains, between 50 and 80 percent of the settlements were destroyed. In the forested areas, in the mountains and in Transdanubia the demographic [population] loss is estimated at 25–30 percent.[10]

Eventually, due to problems back home, the Mongols withdrew as suddenly as they had come. They left behind a wrecked countryside and population, and King Bela faced a monumental task of reconstruction. The king recruited the nobles help by giving them crown lands (lands that belonged to the king). He allowed them to construct castles on their land that would withstand future enemy sieges. To rebuild the population and establish stronger defenses, King Bela turned royal castles into fortified towns and populated them with immigrants, particularly Germans, Italians, and Jews. In this way, Bela was able to rebuild the country. In the process, however, he also allowed the nobility to develop into a powerful political force.

By the end of the thirteenth century, those nobles were squabbling among themselves. King Bela died in 1270, and in 1301, his successor, Andrew III, also died, leaving no heir. Thus, the Arpad dynasty ended, and a state of anarchy followed as factions of nobles vied for control.

CONTROL BY FOREIGNERS

In 1308, the Hungarian nobility selected the first in a succession of foreign kings, each maternally related to the Arpads. These foreign kings stabilized the nation and ended the state of disorder and violence that had lasted since Andrew's death. Among their most notable achievements, the foreign kings replenished the national treasury by making money in the mining industry. They ran Hungary's mining industry so successfully that, over the next two centuries, the country produced more than a third of Europe's gold and a quarter of its silver. This brought renewed prosperity to Hungary. As a result, new towns grew and cultural activity flourished.

The foreign kings were not without problems, though. In particular, they failed to recognize a growing threat from the East. In 1437, the Ottoman Turks again invaded Hungary.

Rule returned to a Hungarian when Janos Hunyadi became regent (governor) for the heir to the throne; since the heir was an infant, he needed someone to rule for him until he was old

enough to do it himself. Although Hunyadi
never held the title of king, he was a well-
respected leader. His greatest achievement
was defeating the Turkish forces in 1456. The
defeat was so great that it was seventy years
before the Turks again posed a serious threat.

After Hunyadi's death, there was some
dispute over the throne. Officially, Hunyadi's
son Matthias Corvinus became king. But
Frederick of Austria also believed he had a
claim to the Hungarian throne. According to
historian Janos Bak, Matthias made peace
with Frederick with a rather unusual deal:

> Frederick, in 1463, [agreed] to accept a
> compromise: he adopted Matthias as his
> son, . . . and received the right to inherit the
> throne should Matthias die heirless. . . .
> [The agreement] was the first step toward
> the Habsburgs' [Austria's ruling family] acquisition of
> Hungary, which was to last for four hundred years.[11]

Janos Hunyadi saved Hungary from the Turks in 1456.

Matthias was a wise and enlightened king and is often remembered as the greatest ruler of medieval Hungary. Matthias
won the respect of the peasants by treating them with justice
and fairness. His military and political accomplishments were
also significant. However, Matthias is best remembered for
making his court a center of culture and the arts. Under his
rule, the first books were printed in Hungary, and he established the country's second university and a library.

THE HABSBURGS MARRY INTO HUNGARY

Matthias was the last Hungarian king to rule a unified Hungary. After his death, the throne was again in dispute, and the
Hungarians chose Ulaszlo of Poland as king. The Austrians,
having hoped to gain the throne of Hungary based on
Matthias's agreement with Frederick, were angry with his
choice. To soothe their feelings, Ulaszlo agreed to marriages
between members of the Hungarian and Austrian royal families. With these marriages, the powerful Austrian Empire
created a bond with the royal family of Hungary.

In August 1526, a Turkish army of one hundred thousand
soldiers attacked Hungary's small, ill-equipped, and poorly

ANONYMOUS

Much of Hungary's early history was recorded in the twelfth century by a chronicler in the court of King Bela III. This historian signed his works only as P. magister. The Hungarians, however, gave this nameless but important historical figure a name. He is called Anonymous, meaning nameless, and his statue in the city park of Budapest is known as the statue of Anonymous. Thus, in Hungary, when historical writing is said to be by Anonymous, it does not mean that the author is unknown but that it was written by King Bela's court historian.

trained army of twenty-five thousand men at the village of Mohacs in southern Transdanubia. The Hungarians were soundly defeated. The Hungarian king and an estimated twenty thousand bishops, nobles, and soldiers died at Mohacs, leaving the Ottoman Empire in control of southern Hungary. The defeat was a monumental event in Hungarian history. It began a period of foreign domination that would last for almost five centuries.

A DIVIDED COUNTRY

After the battle of Mohacs, the Turks occupied the southern part of the nation. The rest of Hungary was left leaderless. Rival factions of Hungarian nobles elected two kings—Janos Zapolyai, a Hungarian, and Ferdinand of Austria, the first Habsburg to rule in Hungary. Each claimed sovereignty over the entire country, but neither was strong enough to eliminate his rival.

As a result, three different powers grabbed for a portion of the Hungarian prize, and the country was partitioned into three parts. The Habsburgs ruled Royal Hungary, which consisted of counties in the west and north. The Ottoman Turks ruled central and southern Hungary. The third section, the principality of Transylvania, was ruled by Janos Zapolyai as a subordinate state of the Ottoman Empire. This division lasted for 150 years.

HABSBURG RULE

Initially the Hungarians saw Austria as an ally who would help drive the Ottoman Turks from Hungarian soil. That was not Austria's plan, however. It soon became apparent to the Hungarians that Austria was placating the Turks in the south and using Royal Hungary as a buffer zone between Austria and the Ottoman Empire. As a result, Hungarian resentment against the Austrians began to build.

The resentment grew even stronger during the sixteenth century when many Hungarian nobles converted from Catholicism to Protestantism and were persecuted by the Habsburgs for their beliefs. The Habsburgs were strict Catholics and intolerant of any other religion developing in the lands under their control. For this reason, anti-Habsburg feelings had reached the boiling point by the mid-seventeenth century.

In 1681, the Hungarians rebelled against the Habsburgs and won some concessions. However, the conflict once again signaled weakness to the Turks, who attacked Austria. An army of Polish, German, and Austrian forces met the challenge and drove back the invaders. The Turkish forces had pushed too far west and found themselves cut off from their power base.

A groundskeeper works amongst the carved wooden poles that commemorate Hungary's devastating defeat by the Turks in 1526.

This win was significant for Hungary. Over the next two decades, the combined armies of the countries that made up the Holy Roman Empire also weakened the Turkish hold on central and southern Hungary. And in 1699 the Turkish occupation ended with the Peace of Karlowitz.

DEEPENING HOSTILITY

Following the defeat of the Turks, the victorious Habsburgs extended their rule to all of Hungary, and the country became an Austrian colony. The Hungarians, though, resented having their defense, tariffs, and other government functions controlled by Austria. These feelings intensified, and, in 1703, Transylvanian prince Ferenc Rakoczi started a rebellion that for the first time united Hungarians against the Habsburgs. After eight years, though, the rebellion ended in defeat. The Hungarians gained little following Rakoczi's rebellion and their dislike of Austrian rule continued.

In 1711, Habsburg ruler Charles VI came to power. Desiring peace in his domain, Charles made an effort to improve the relationship between Hungary and Austria. He modernized Hungary's government administration and established a standing army. However, Charles created new resentments by limiting the religious freedom of the Hungarian people. He banned their conversion to Protestantism, required all civil servants to be Catholic, and forbade Protestants to study abroad.

MARIA THERESA

When Charles died in 1740, his twenty-three-year-old daughter, Maria Theresa, took the throne. Maria Theresa was the first Habsburg ruler to make an honest attempt to address the Hungarians' concerns, although she did so only in return for Hungary's military assistance.

During the mid-eighteenth century, Frederick, the ruler of nearby Prussia, thinking that the young Maria Theresa would be a weak ruler, tried to seize some of the Habsburg's territory. Frederick underestimated the new empress, however. Instead of losing Austrian territory, Maria Theresa made a personal appeal to the Hungarians and won that nation's support in her battle against Prussia. The combined Austrian and Hungarian armies defeated Prussia in 1748.

Maria Theresa rewarded the Hungarians by agreeing to some concessions. For example, she admitted Hungarian nobles to posts in her government and allowed them to send their sons to the Theresianum, an academy she founded in Vienna for the sons of the aristocracy. And for the lesser nobles, she founded the Royal Hungarian Bodyguard, an organization to which each Hungarian county sent two youths of noble birth for military training.

REBELLION

Despite Maria Theresa's efforts, tension between the Austrian Empire and its subject country continued to grow, and several Hungarians emerged as political leaders. One of the first, Istvan Szechenyi, supported economic reform but favored maintaining a strong link with the Habsburg Empire. Another popular reform leader, Lajos Kossuth, disagreed. Kossuth believed that Hungary should be independent, and he argued that only political and economic separation from Austria would solve the country's problems.

Lajos Kossuth believed Hungary should be an independent country.

In March 1848, peasants in Vienna, Austria, rioted and demanded better wages, better housing, and a voice in their own affairs. The rebellion distracted Austria's leaders from the problems in Hungary, and the Hungarians saw this as an opportunity. On March 15, Hungarian poet Sandor Petofi led a group of radicals and students into the streets to call for revolution. Because of its internal problems, Austria had little time to deal with the Hungarian rebellion. Within days, the rebels declared a new national government, with Kossuth as its provisional head.

Their apparent victory, however, was short-lived. In December 1848, eighteen-year-old Francis Joseph became emperor of Austria. The young emperor showed little patience in dealing with the Hungarian revolt. In June 1849, he requested help from Austria's allies, the Russians, who sent two hundred thousand troops to attack Hungary from the east. By August, the Hungarians surrendered, and Austrian rule was restored.

Following the defeat, Francis Joseph treated Hungary harshly. He had many of the Hungarian leaders executed.

Others, including Kossuth, fled the country, and Petofi died in battle.

THE AUSTRO-HUNGARIAN EMPIRE

By the mid-1860s, however, Francis Joseph's hold on his empire was weakening. For years Austria had faced both internal strife and confrontations with other European nations. Francis Joseph realized he needed Hungary's cooperation to reassert Austria's position as leader in Europe. To gain Hungary's cooperation, Francis Joseph agreed to the Compromise of 1867, which created the Dual Monarchy of Austria-Hungary, also known as the Austro-Hungarian Empire. Under this agreement, Francis Joseph reigned as emperor of Austria and king of Hungary. But the compromise allowed Hungary more control over its internal affairs than at any time since the 1526 Turkish victory at Mohacs. Defense and foreign relations were shared, but Hungary gained its own prime minister and parliament and control over domestic affairs.

Over the next fifty years, Hungarian society prospered. Industry and trade developed rapidly, and the railway network increased in size. Hungary's social and economic systems also began to change. The country became less agricultural and more industrial. By 1900, 13 percent of the population was employed in mines and industry, and a strong working class was developing. However, the peasantry and industrial workers still had almost no political rights, and discontent was growing.

The beginning of World War I pushed the impending internal conflict into the background. On June 28, 1914, Archduke Francis Ferdinand, heir to the Austrian throne, was assassinated in Sarajevo, Bosnia, by a Serbian man. A month later, Austrian emperor Francis Joseph declared war on Serbia. By August 1914, the Austro-Hungarian Empire was at the heart of a war that involved all of Europe.

THE UNCONQUERABLE SOUL OF HUNGARY

When Austria declared war on Serbia in 1914, Hungary, as part of the Dual Monarchy, was forced into the fight. By late summer, almost all of Europe was at war. In Budapest, bands played military music, and patriotic demonstrators filled the streets. Spirits were high, and everyone expected a quick and easy victory. No one dreamed that the six-hundred-year-old Habsburg dynasty would collapse, or that Hungary would begin another long period of anarchy, political repression, and poverty before finally becoming its own master.

WORLD WAR I

As the war dragged on, victory for the Dual Monarchy slipped farther out of reach. The Allies (Great Britain, France, Russia, and the United States) were winning considerable territory, and the citizens of the Austro-Hungarian Empire suffered widespread food shortages and high inflation. Then, in 1916, Francis Joseph, emperor of Austria and king of Hungary, died. His successor, Charles IV (1916–1918) was a well-meaning man, but he lacked the strength to lead an empire through a war more costly in terms of money and human life than any the world had ever seen.

By late 1918, the cost to Hungary had become crippling. Farm and factory production had dropped to half of the pre-war level. Almost two-thirds of the 3.6 million soldiers Hungary sent to war were killed or wounded, and the Hungarian people had lost all hope of victory.

In October 1918, dissatisfaction with the war and the Austro-Hungarian leadership finally erupted into revolution in Budapest. Hungarian prime minister Istvan Tisza was assassinated, and Mihaly Karolyi, leader of the anti-German opposition in parliament, became prime minister. The new government dissolved the parliament, pronounced Hungary an independent republic no longer under Austrian rule, and tried to make peace with the Allies. The Hungarians hoped that by abandoning Austria and Germany, they would win favor with the victorious powers and be allowed to retain control over all of the territory they held before the war. Shortly before assuming leadership of the country, Karolyi said, "We have lost the war, what is important now is to make certain that we do not lose the peace."[12]

This was not to be. Instead, the 1920 Treaty of Trianon, the treaty that dealt with Hungary's participation in the war, punished Hungary severely, taking two-thirds of the country's land and three-fifths of its population. The largest single loss was Transylvania. Its approximately sixty-three thousand square miles and almost 2 million people went to Romania. Czechoslovakia and Yugoslavia also gained large tracts of Hungarian land, and Austria, Poland, and Italy received small parcels. As Karolyi feared, Hungary lost the peace as well as the war, and the country was stunned by the magnitude of the loss.

A KINGDOM WITHOUT A KING

Political, economic, and social turmoil reigned in Hungary after World War I. Hungary was still officially a monarchy, but the dissolution of the Habsburg dynasty left it with no king, and one was not immediately chosen. Instead, the parliament chose Admiral Miklos Horthy, a former navy officer, to head the country as regent until a new king was named. Horthy served as regent throughout the twenty-one years between the first and second world wars.

Horthy's government proved to be extremely conservative and right wing. Although it advocated traditional values supporting family, state, and religion, the standard of living of the workers and peasants remained poor. Wages were lower than prewar levels, and the peasants had no political voice.

In 1929, the New York Stock Exchange crashed, dealing a crippling blow to Hungary's already weak economy. Following the stock market crash, world grain prices plummeted, presenting Hungary with another serious problem since grain was an important Hungarian export. The loss of income from grain exports was a further blow to the struggling economy.

The Hungarians were desperately looking for ways to solve the problems that had plagued them since the end of World War I. Thinking the return of the lost territories would

Admiral Miklos Horthy served as Hungary's regent for twenty-one years.

solve the nation's economic and political woes, Horthy looked to the growing fascist government of Germany's Adolf Hitler for help in reclaiming the lost lands.

A PRICE TO PAY

Hitler's support came with a high price tag, however. Using promises, economic pressure, and the threat of military intervention, Hitler convinced Horthy's government to adopt the policies of his Nazi regime. Those policies included Hitler's brutal treatment of Jews.

THE TREATY OF TRIANON

The Treaty of Trianon, reluctantly signed by Hungary after World War I, dealt harshly with Hungary's participation in the war. The treaty, sometimes referred to by Hungarians as the Shame of Trianon, reduced the size of Hungary by about two-thirds. Areas populated largely by nationalities other than ethnic Magyars were parceled out to Hungary's neighbors, but many Magyars found themselves displaced as well. The regions of Ruthenia, in modern-day Ukraine, and Slovakia became part of Czechoslovakia. Yugoslavia gained Croatia, Slavonia, and part of the Banat (an agricultural region in the Danube basin). Austria was given Burgenland. Transylvania, with its 2 million Magyars, went to Romania. In all, after the Treaty of Trianon, about three-fifths of the Hungarian population, including 3 million ethnic Magyars, lived outside of their homeland.

In addition to the huge loss of land and people, Hungary lost its access to the sea and most of its natural resources. Hungary lost 84 percent of its timber resources, 43 percent of its land suitable for farming, and 83 percent of its iron ore. Because the nation's prewar industry was concentrated around Budapest, Hungary did retain more than half of its industry. However, with the loss of so many natural resources, industry was separated from its source of raw materials.

Hungarians were deeply disturbed by the terms of the treaty. Even today, more than eighty years later, the Treaty of Trianon remains an open wound for most Hungarians. It still colors their political views and their relationship with neighboring countries.

Before the alliance with Adolf Hitler, Jews were not seen as social equals by many Hungarians, but overall they were accepted. Further, according to Stephen Burant, editor of *Hungary: A Country Study*, Hungary's relatively small Jewish population played an important role in the nation's economy. Burant writes:

The 1930 census showed that Jews made up only 5.1 percent of the population but provided 54.5 percent of its [Hungary's] physicians, 31.7 percent of its journalists, and 49.2 percent of its lawyers. Jews controlled an estimated 19.5 percent to 33 percent of the national income, four of the five leading banks, and 80 percent of Hungary's industry.[13]

In spite of the Jews' significant economic contributions, many Hungarians, caught up in the wave of anti-Semitism sweeping Europe, found the Jewish population to be an easy scapegoat. The primary anti-Semitic voice in Hungary was the Arrow Cross Party, Hungary's equivalent of Germany's Nazi Party. Like the Nazis, the Arrow Cross promised a more stable and affluent economy to a disillusioned society. Desperate to improve their quality of life, Hungarians listened, and the party gained support.

As a result, discrimination against Hungary's Jews increased dramatically. At first, many jobs were no longer available to Jews, and they were not welcome in many places of business. Soon the discrimination escalated to imprisonment and deportation, and culminated in the summer of 1944, when four hundred thousand Hungarian Jewish men, women, and children were deported to labor camps in Germany and Austria. There, many were murdered or died of disease.

Hungarian Jews were subject to discrimination, imprisonment, and deportation during World War II.

A HERO'S STORY

In 1944, the Swedish government sent Raoul Wallenberg, a member of a wealthy and influential family, on a diplomatic assignment to Budapest. Wallenberg, a gentile, was instructed to save as many Hungarian Jews as possible from Adolf Hitler's concentration camps.

Wallenberg brought to the task business and organizational ability as well as personal charm and negotiating skills. He was often seen in congenial company with Nazi officials. While he was shaking hands and smiling with the Germans, however, he was busy devising ingenious ways to save more lives. He created special Swedish passports to give Jews immunity from Nazi atrocities. He opened safe houses where Jews were protected from Nazi interference. He even personally stopped trains heading for the concentration camps and demanded the release of hundreds of Jews whom he insisted fell under the protection of the Swedish government. He cajoled, bribed, intimidated, lied—whatever it took—to save an estimated thirty thousand Jews from the death camps.

Anticipating Hitler's impending defeat, Wallenberg hoped to start an organization that would help Jews regain their property and find jobs and homes. He was eager to meet with the Soviets, who occupied Hungary in 1945, and make arrangements for establishing his Jewish relief organization. On January 17, 1945, Wallenberg left his office to meet with the Russians and was never heard from again. No one knows why the Russians would have wanted to arrest him, but for years there were vague reports that he had been seen in various Russian prisons. However, no contact was ever reliably confirmed. As late as 2001, a new investigation was held to try to learn what happened to Raoul Wallenberg. The Russians finally admitted that he had been arrested, but shed no light on his eventual fate. Whatever his fate, Raoul Wallenberg will always be remembered as a hero by Hungarian Jews.

DRAWN INTO ANOTHER WORLD WAR

Still hoping to regain lost territory and rebuild its economy, in 1939 Hungary followed Germany into World War II, fighting against the Allied powers—the Soviet Union, Great Britain, France, and later the United States. The war did not go well for Hungary. Even though Hungary could not meet the economic needs of its own people, Germany demanded increased amounts of food, forced labor, and soldiers to support the war. Ultimately, the increased demands, plus more than one hundred thousand Hungarian casualties at the 1942–1943 battle of Stalingrad in the Soviet Union, again pushed the Hungarian government to begin secret negotiations with the Allies. Hitler suspected the negotiations, however. He feared that Hungary might make a separate peace with the Allies, and worried he would lose the Hungarian food and labor. Therefore, in 1943, Nazi forces occupied Hungary and forced the government to further increase its contribution to the German war effort.

Following the Nazi occupation, Hungary became an international battleground. In 1944, Soviet troops advanced into Hungary from the east, forcing the German army to retreat. As they left, the German army demolished Hungary's road, rail, and communication systems. They wanted to leave nothing that would be of use to the Allied forces.

On April 4, 1945, the last of the German army left Hungary. The Allies had won the war, and the Soviets, the first of the Allies to invade Hungary, took control of a country in a state of chaos.

LIFE BEHIND THE IRON CURTAIN

After World War II, the Soviet Union subverted attempts at democracy and gradually installed its own communist political, social, and economic system in Hungary and the rest of Eastern Europe. Hungary, and the other Eastern European countries now under Soviet domination, became known as the Communist or Eastern bloc and were described as existing behind an iron curtain—meaning they were economically and politically cut off from the Western world.

After the war, creating jobs and stabilizing the economy were of the utmost importance in Europe. In Hungary, as in most Eastern bloc countries, new labor and building jobs were created by postwar reconstruction, and administrative and clerical jobs were needed to support the vast bureaucracy required to run the Communist system. Jobs were also created by the Soviet industrial philosophy, which emphasized heavy industry such as steel production rather than the production of consumer goods. As a result, the shortage of both luxury items and basic household goods grew.

Although new jobs were created, private ownership of businesses was almost completely taken away from the people. The new Soviet-controlled government nationalized banking, trade, and industry. Even the farms no longer belonged to individual families. Farmers were forced to pool their land and resources into collective farms and to deliver farm products to the government at prices that were often lower than the cost of production. Thus, by 1949, 99 percent of Hungary's workers, whether on farms or in factories, were state employees.

During the first years of communism, the economy blossomed. People worked for the government rather than for private owners, but unemployment was low. And, in spite of shortages of many consumer goods, especially luxury items, the standard of living improved because everyone had a job and the government provided many social services such as health care, education, and subsidized vacations. This improved economy caused many Hungarians to embrace the

Residents walk a war-ravaged street in Budapest in 1945. At the end of World War II, the Soviet Union took control of Hungary.

ideals of communism and become loyal members of the Communist Party.

The Communists presented their system as an ideal that would create a worker's paradise for the Hungarian people. Everyone would share in the population's collective productivity. In theory, Hungarian Communists would also participate in their government. In reality, however, this was not the case. No decision could be made without the approval of the Soviets. Therefore, as time went on, Hungarians began to realize that communism could not deliver the worker's paradise it promised, and many people began to resent the strict governmental control over their lives.

The Soviet Union established a communist system in Hungary nationalizing industries such as agriculture.

THE HATED AVO

The Hungarian people had endured varying degrees of hardship and domination by foreign powers through most of their history. So, in spite of being disappointed by the realities of communism, they might have settled comfortably into the new system. However, one organization, sanctioned by the Soviets, but made up of Hungarian citizens, made life intolerable.

The Allamvedelmi Osztaly (AVO) was a secret police force comprised of Hungarian citizens. It was originally organized as a division of the state police; later it became a special department answerable only to the top Communist leaders. The organizers of this force recruited people with no family or close ties, believing that would make them less likely to be lenient with their fellow Hungarian citizens.

Although the AVO was organized under the direction and watchful eye of its Soviet masters, its final form was probably more powerful than the Soviets originally planned. The AVO had the authority to arrest Hungarian citizens on minor charges or no charges at all. AVO officers could beat and torture people before sending them to prisons, where many died from the brutal treatment they received. AVO spies, often recruited through blackmail and threats, were everywhere—in the workplace, in the neighborhood, and sometimes in families. Even schoolchildren were taught to report on their parents. Journalist Endre Marton (who survived eighteen months in an AVO prison) describes the AVO:

> The secret police became the real power throughout the land, a state within the state, feared even by the Hungarian communists. . . . The [AVO] developed an army of its own. It set up watchtowers, minefields, and barbed wire fences along the borders. This military array was the visible evidence of [AVO] power. Undercover, thousands of other secret police officers penetrated every nook of Hungarian life. They spied, reported, kidnapped, imprisoned, and murdered countless thousands of their fellow citizens. No outsider knew exactly how many men Peter [Gabor, head of the AVO] had under his command at his peak. One accepted figure was eighty thousand, not counting thousands of occasional agents and informants. This was a huge force in a coun-

try smaller than the state of Kentucky, with fewer than ten million Magyars [Hungarians].[14]

THE PEOPLE REBEL

The political control exercised by the Soviets, combined with the power of the AVO, became increasingly intolerable. As a result, the writers of Hungary began writing about the growing desire for change. Soon they had a following of university students who formed the Unified Organization of Hungarian University and College Students, a political student organization.

The students and writers were not content just to criticize the government. They took action. They printed and distributed a list of their demands and planned a public rally. Their demands consisted of sixteen points beginning with the immediate evacuation of all Soviet troops and ballot elections of all new public officials. They also asked for freedom of speech, expression, and the press. Other points included issues such as reorganization of the Soviet economic system and free trade. The writers and students were not asking for

The AVO were so hated that members were arrested at gunpoint during the Revolt of 1956.

TWO REFUGEES

Following the 1956 revolt, many Hungarians fled the country to avoid being arrested or to seek a better life. Zoltan Bush and his fiancée, Vickie, were two of them.

Zoltan Bush, an engineering student and a professional soccer player, had been identified as a "suspicious person," a phrase that allowed the AVO to arrest people without a specific charge. Initially Bush was sent to a state labor camp, where he worked until a secretary told him she had typed his name on a list. He did not know what crime he was accused of, but he knew what being "on a list" meant. His next stop would be prison, unless he could escape across the Yugoslavian border near his home in southern Hungary.

Bush's escape route lay across a snow-covered field patrolled by armed border guards. More than forty years later, Zoltan Bush still remembers the fear of stepping into that snowy field right under the noses of the guards. He recalls that he felt as exposed as "a cockroach on a white tablecloth" as he walked out into the white field wearing a long black overcoat. Even more clearly, he remembers the emptiness of walking away from his home, family, and fiancée.

After he made it safely to a Yugoslavian refugee camp, Bush sent a message to his worried family. The message said that the tennis shoes had arrived, a code to let his family know he was safe. His fiancée, eighteen-year-old Vickie, sent a return message saying that she would send his boots soon, meaning that she would soon join him.

It was midsummer before the "boots" could arrange to join the "tennis shoes." When the time came, a farmer covered Vickie and a friend with a tarp and drove them to the border in his horse-drawn cart after dark. The two then crept into a cornfield and waited for a chance to run for the Yugoslavian border. In a May 2001 interview with the author, Vickie Bush remembers the heat and

> hundreds of mosquitoes. Finally, we just couldn't stand it any longer. The mosquitoes seemed almost worse than the bullets, so we made a run for a tree that we believed to be on Yugoslavian soil. As we crouched under the tree and caught our breath, we heard a snick, and I felt a gun barrel pressed to my head. What a relief when the guard spoke to us in Yugoslavian!

Eventually, Zoltan and Vickie joined Zoltan's brother and his American wife in the United States. Today, all four live in Panama City, Florida.

Forradalmi kormányt

an end to communism, but the end of Soviet domination and a reorganized Communist government.

The writers and students publicized their demands at a rally on October 23, 1956, in Budapest. However, what began as a peaceful, but noisy, demonstration turned violent when the AVO fired on an unarmed group of students gathered outside a radio station. Noel Barber, a journalist who covered the rally and the events that followed, describes the scene after the AVO began firing:

A leader of the uprising stands behind the Hungarian nationalist flag as he recites the demands for freedom of speech and expression.

> The shrieks of fear gave way to a sullen muttering against the secret police until the street was alive with one cry, "Death to the Avo!" The crowd could just make out the Avos on the rooftops or leaning out of upper

windows, guns pointed to the street, safe against an unarmed crowd that could only hurl bricks in impotent
rage. "I will always remember one split second," Anna
[a demonstrator] continues. "The sight of two Avos at a
window pointing downwards and laughing."[15]

A CRY FOR HELP

The students and others assembled and fought back with
rocks, sticks, bottle bombs, and other homemade weapons.
The Revolt of 1956 had begun. Factory workers who had been
staunch Communist Party members joined the students. The
army was called out to control the rebellion, but many soldiers
instead joined the uprising, bringing their weapons with
them. On October 24, Soviet troops entered the city to break
up the riots. Their presence just made the crowds angrier.

For a few days victory seemed within reach. On Wednes-
day, October 24, Imre Nagy, a political leader who enjoyed
popular support, was named prime minister of a new government consisting of both communist and noncommunist
members. He dissolved the state security police, abolished
the one-party system, and promised free elections.

However, the victory was an illusion. Before dawn on
November 4, 1956, Soviet troops, tanks, and warplanes
launched a powerful attack on Hungary. It was still dark
when Imre Nagy spoke to his compatriots on the radio. He
announced: "Today at daybreak, Soviet troops attacked our
capital with the obvious intent of overthrowing the legal
Hungarian democratic government. Our troops are in com-
bat; the government is at its post. I notify the people of our
country and the entire world of this fact."[16]

Hungary asked the United Nations and Western governments for protection, but got no help. Later in the day, an
unidentified radio announcer made an impassioned plea to
the world as the battle raged outside the broadcasting station. The announcer said:

> Civilized people of the world, in the name of liberty and
> solidarity [unity], we are asking you to help. Our ship is
> sinking. The light vanishes. The shadows grow darker
> from hour to hour. Listen to our cry. Start moving. Ex-
> tend to us brotherly hands. People of the world, save us.
> S-O-S. Help, help, help. God be with you and with us.[17]

The Soviet military launched a merciless offensive to quell the uprising on November 4, 1956, including a pre-dawn tank attack on Budapest.

Help did not come, though, and the Soviet military quickly quelled the revolt, leaving twenty-five thousand people dead.

Even though it was not successful, the Hungarian revolt and a less violent workers' revolt in Poland sent a message to the world that the Soviet-controlled Eastern bloc was not a worker's paradise as the Soviets had claimed. Barber wrote:

The uprising was not in vain. For a few glorious days it gave notice to the free world that the Hungarian pen was mightier than the Soviet sword. And it proved something else: that even when the youth of a country is indoctrinated for years, when it is handpicked almost from birth to be trained as tomorrow's Communist elite, no alien master can obliterate the desire for freedom that lies in everyone. It needed only a spark—provided by the

LOSSES OF THE BRAIN DRAIN

In 1956, following the failed Hungarian revolution, writer James Michener was on hand to assist Hungarian refugees fleeing to Austria and to record their stories in his book *The Bridge at Andau*. To illustrate the drain losing so many citizens had on Hungarian human resources, he describes eleven groups who made up part of the two hundred thousand who fled their homeland in the weeks following the revolution:

One, at the university in Sopron five hundred students, thirty-two professors and their entire families simply gave up all hope of a decent life under communism and came across the border. . . .

Two, the finest ballerina of the Budapest Opera walked out with several of her assistants.

Three, enough football [soccer] players fled Hungary to make several teams of world-champion caliber.

Four, the three finest Gypsy orchestras of Hungary came out in a body and have begun to play around the restaurants of Europe.

Five, some of the top mechanics in the factories at Csepel [an industrial area in Budapest] left and were eagerly grabbed up by firms in Germany, Switzerland and Sweden.

Six, a staggering number of trained engineers and scientists in almost all phases of industry and research fled. . . .

Seven, a majority of both the Budapest symphony orchestras came out. . . . Several of the best conductors came with them.

Eight, many of Hungary's best artists crossed the border.

Nine, and many of her notable writers.

Ten, several members of the Hungarian Olympic team decided to stay in Australia [where the 1956 Olympics were held], others defected along the way home. . . .

Eleven, and most impressive of all, were the young couples with babies.

writers—to send the youngsters of Hungary in their thousands to man the barricades, to fight and often to die in an uprising of youth triumphant.[18]

THE AFTERMATH

Hungary paid a high price for the attempt to end Soviet domination. About two hundred thousand of Hungary's youngest and brightest citizens fled across the Austrian and Yugoslavian borders to escape imprisonment or execution by the reinstated Communist government. Many died in the attempt. Even as the refugees fled, the Communists began a campaign of reprisals. Over the next five years, about two thousand participants in the revolution, including Imre Nagy, were executed, and another twenty-five thousand were imprisoned.

However, the failed revolution sent a message to the Soviet-controlled government that the Hungarian people would rather fight than accept a return to total Soviet control. As a result, the Soviets agreed to make some compromises and implement some reforms, such as permitting some elements of democracy to coexist with the Communist system.

JANOS KADAR

On November 4, 1956, Janos Kadar, a powerful Hungarian politician controlled by the Soviets, became head of the Hungarian government. Kadar's new government implemented a series of reforms that softened Hungary's rigid Communist economy and introduced elements of a free market. More trade with countries outside of the Eastern bloc was allowed, and some Hungarians were even allowed to open small businesses.

Thanks to Kadar's system of communism, by the 1970s Hungary was far ahead of the other Communist bloc countries in standard of living and freedom of movement and speech. Speech was still controlled, but Hungarians were allowed to express political opinions more openly than in the past. And, although there were still shortages, many consumer goods were more readily available than they had been since before World War II. Consequently, Hungary became a model among Eastern bloc countries and attracted much Western attention and investment.

Some historians see the changes and successes as superficial, however. The Hungarian people still lived under an oppressive political system in which they had no voice. Macartney, for one, considers the policy changes to be little more than cosmetic. He writes:

> Personal freedoms were larger, more contact with the West allowed, more production of consumer goods permitted and the economic exchanges with the U.S.S.R. made less inequitable. But no concession was made on fundamentals, and the Hungarian people remained the prisoners of that East on which they had turned their backs when Arpad led them across the Carpathians, more than 1,000 years ago.[19]

AN ERA ENDS QUIETLY

Soviet control of Hungary ended in 1989 when the Communist system collapsed in the Soviet Union. The reasons for the collapse included a declining economy, decades of industrial and agricultural pollution, increased public health problems,

Janos Kadar (left) and Soviet premier Nikita Khrushchev, at a ceremony in Budapest.

TRAITOR OR PATRIOT?

Communist leader Janos Kadar is seen by some as Hungary's greatest patriot and by others as its worst traitor. Kadar, who, in the early days of communism, was involved in the arrests, trials, and executions of many of his own close colleagues, was himself arrested in 1951 for unknown reasons. After the Revolt of 1956, he did an apparent about-face in political strategy. He appeared to have abandoned his ruthless tactics in order to lead Hungary into a more open, less restrictive political life. However, new evidence shows that Kadar secretly continued his old tactics and was personally involved in the execution of many leaders of the failed revolution, including Imre Nagy, the people's choice to lead the country after the revolution.

Kadar still has the power to arouse strong emotions among his fellow Hungarians. Some Hungarians revere him for his contributions to improving life under communism after the 1956 revolt, while others hate him for the cruelty he is reputed to have shown his fellow Hungarians.

and a declining life expectancy. The Soviets had lost control of their empire. According to writer Robert Paxton:

> Three generations of Soviet citizens had sacrificed liberty in exchange for the promise of equitably distributed abundance. When they realized that they could expect only shoddy and scarce goods for the rest of their lives, cynicism and corruption spread widely under a façade of Communist conformity.[20]

In September 1989, Hungary cut down the barbed-wire barrier marking its border with Austria, a nation outside of the Eastern bloc. The so-called iron curtain that had kept the Eastern bloc isolated from the rest of Europe had been breached. Almost immediately, the Communist governments in Hungary and the other Soviet satellites collapsed. Hungary, once again, became an independent nation with the freedom to choose its own form of government. Soviet rule, a period the Hungarians now call *az atkos 40 ev* (the accursed forty years) was over. Hungary was finally master of its own fate.

4
FROM COMMUNISM TO THE EUROPEAN UNION

The fall of the iron curtain left Hungary and the other former Communist bloc countries exposed to the eyes of the world. The world waited to see how these nations would react to free choice. Many people in capitalist societies expected the former Communist nations to embrace capitalism and democracy with enthusiasm. For many Hungarians, though, it was Soviet repression they had disliked, not the Communist economic system and form of government. Thus, many hesitated to give up the security of communism, while others wanted to rush into capitalism. The important thing, though, was that the choice was finally in the hands of the voters. In October 1989, Hungary changed its name back to its pre-World War II name, the Republic of Hungary. As members of a republic, Hungarians would have the right and responsibility to form political parties and elect leaders.

NEW POLITICAL PARTIES EMERGE
Because of the government reforms that began after the 1956 revolution, Hungary was ahead of its neighbors in making the switch to a market economy (an economic system based on prices for goods set by buyers and sellers) and a democratic political system. Even so, the changeover has proved difficult.

For decades the Communist Party had been the only political party allowed in Hungary. After 1989, though, people had a choice. Many of these people resented the repression of the Communist era and were ready for political change. Communist Party leaders knew they would have to make the party image more appealing in order to remain a force in national politics. The party changed its name to the Hungarian Socialist Party (MSZP). The reorganized party favored a social democracy that would combine elements of communism and democracy. However, forty years of heavy-handed rule was not easily forgotten, and opposition parties quickly organized.

Every ideological variation soon unveiled its own political party. The cautious Hungarian Democratic Forum (MDF), for example, supported a gradual transition to capitalism. The Social-Democratic Alliance of Free Democrats (SZDSZ) favored much more rapid change. Many other smaller parties espoused other goals and political platforms, and no one party had a majority. According to writer Janos Dobszay, the varying ideologies made compromise in forming a new government difficult:

> One of the reasons for the increasing roughness of Hungarian political life was that arguments on facts and sober considerations were replaced by pledges of allegiance to various political flags, . . . based on a belief that the party or fraction they stood for embodied the true faith. . . . As a result, . . . it was often impossible to resolve practical questions without debates on ideology.[21]

The number of small parties and the initial unwillingness to compromise made electing a new government difficult. However, compromises were finally reached and in 1990 the MDF formed a coalition government with two smaller parties, the

Viktor Orban formed a coalition government after being elected prime minister in 1998.

Independent Smallholders' Party (FKgP) and the Christian Democrats (KDNP). The coalition provided Hungary with a sound government during the initial period of transition from communism to capitalism.

ON THE THRESHOLD OF A NEW MILLENNIUM

Today Hungary has a stable government elected by the people. The modern government consists of a prime minister, fourteen ministries, or departments, and a parliament. Parliament is unicameral, or consisting of one legislative branch, and has 386 seats. Viktor Orban was elected prime minister in the 1998 election, but no party won a majority of votes. Therefore, the newly elected prime minister formed a coalition government made up of the three strongest parties—the Fidexz–MPP, the Independent Smallholders' Party, and the Hungarian Democratic Forum.

With his new government program titled "On the Threshold of a New Millennium," Viktor Orban promised to tailor his government to serve the Hungarian citizens. According to a fact sheet issued by the Ministry of Foreign Affairs, Orban's government intends to

> build on the accomplishments of previous Governments . . . to guide Hungary's social development in such a way that each citizen will have the chance to enjoy genuine freedom and prosperity; . . . and where the initiative and creative power of individuals and communities will be encouraged and developed; and where we will be able to achieve the ultimate goal of Hungarian politics since 1989: the creation of a civic Hungary.[22]

STRIVING FOR EUROPEAN UNION STANDARDS

Hungary sees membership in the alliance of European nations called the European Union (EU) as a vital step toward realizing the government's goals. The EU currently includes fifteen Western European countries, but it is considering opening membership to several Eastern European countries as well. Hungary hopes to be among the first new members accepted, and its government is focused on meeting the stringent standards set by the EU for new members.

The EU has several goals. It seeks to simplify business transactions among member nations, strengthen Europe's place in world markets by integrating the economies of the European member nations, and introduce a common currency called the Euro. EU members also join forces in matters such as security, foreign policy, economic controls, human rights, and environmental protection.

Each member nation has an equal voice in the operation of the EU. The presidency of the EU rotates every six months among the member countries. Representatives of the member nations also meet every six months to consider current issues. A European parliament is elected by the member nations, and there is a Court of Justice to settle disputes involving member states, businesses, individuals, or EU institutions. In 2001, the EU had fifteen full members: Austria, Belgium, Britain, Denmark, Finland, France, Germany, Greece, Ireland, Italy, Luxembourg, the Netherlands, Portugal, Spain, and Sweden.

EU membership is attractive to small nations because, as a large conglomerate, the EU has more negotiating power in world markets than independent nations. Additionally, a combined Europe can provide better defensive measures and carry more weight in other world organizations such as the United Nations. Therefore, thirteen Central and Eastern European candidates, including Hungary, have applied for EU membership. In order to be accepted, though, prospective members must meet tough standards in a number of areas including economy, agriculture, human rights, and environmental protection.

Hungary is taking aggressive steps to meet these standards. EU leaders predict that the EU may welcome the first wave of new members as early as 2004. Hungary has difficult issues to resolve, such as agricultural problems and immigration policies. However, in some areas, such as developing a strong market economy, Hungary has made a favorable impression and is on the fast track toward being one of the first new members accepted.

DEVELOPING A STRONG MARKET ECONOMY

After some initial successes, Hungary's economy went into a slump following the 1989 changeover. Hungarians had expected the conversion to a market economy to make fast improvements in their living standards and were disappointed with the reality. Under communism, unemployment had been virtually nonexistent, but under capitalism, the unemployment rate rose to 11 percent. As a result, the general attitude of the population became pessimistic. In a 1995 poll only 14 percent of Hungarians were satisfied with the country's post-Communist economic and political course.

There were a number of causes for the problems with the transition process. For one, the Hungarian population was accustomed to an authoritarian government and had no experience with freedom and responsibility. Hungarians had accepted the Communist's governmental paternalism and preferred it to risk taking and the assumption of individual responsibility. Journalist Gyorgy Csepeli writes: "What developed [under Communist rule] was a sort of learned helplessness that made it impossible for the individual to believe in the possibility of controlling his or her own destiny through internalized drives, such as motivation, effort, knowledge or skills."[23]

Further, because most of the country's workforce had never lived in a noncommunist society, adjusting to the responsibilities and freedoms of a democracy was difficult. Under communism, everyone had a job, and many social services such as health care, child care, and even some entertainment opportunities were provided by the government. The worker had few decisions to make and did not have to take responsibility for his own welfare.

However, the Hungarians, who have a lengthy history of surviving adversity, made the necessary adjustments and are slowly improving their economy. In a speech on national television, Hungarian prime minister Viktor Orban said, "Hungary was a loser in the 20th century but will be a winner in the 21st. . . . The dominant twin virtues of the 21st century will be entrepreneurial spirit and perseverance at work, where Hungarians have already proved their excellence."[24]

Orban's optimism is based on a wave of economic success that began as the twentieth century ended and seemed to be gaining momentum in the twenty-first. By 1999, economic growth was considerable. In spite of an economic slowdown in the EU, Hungary's gross domestic product (GDP—the total value of the annual output of goods and services produced within a nation's borders) grew by 4.3 percent that year, twice the average rate of Western European countries. The growth in 2000 was even more impressive at 5.3 percent.

The economic upturn heralded the creation of new jobs and growth in employment. In 1999, for example, employment went up 3.1 percent. Much of the improvement came where it was most needed, in regions with the highest unemployment rates.

IMMIGRATION CONCERNS

Despite Hungary's progress in building a strong economy, there are still areas that must be improved in order to meet EU standards. Several issues in particular are contributing to disagreement and endless debate between Hungary and the EU.

The question of free movement of labor across borders, for instance, has generated much discussion and dissension between EU members and the new candidates. Some Western European countries, especially those located along the borders with Eastern Europe, fear that a flood of immigrant

labor will overwhelm their economies when the EU doors open to new members. After much debate, these fears were eased in late 2001 by a regulation that gives individual countries the right to regulate immigration across their own borders for the first seven years after new members are accepted. Most EU members are satisfied with the new regulation. They anticipate it working well and say they will regulate the movement of people only if excessive immigration puts stress on their economy.

Workers talk outside a steel plant in Western Transdanubia. The steel industry has been a successful component of Hungary's post-Soviet economy.

Due to confidence in the continued growth of its economy, Hungary does not believe the immigration concerns pose a problem. Hungarian prime minister Viktor Orban claims that EU countries have no reason to fear a flood of Hungarian workers when Hungary joins the EU. In fact, Orban believes that with Hungary's surging economic growth, workers will want to move into Hungary rather than out. To support this assertion, Orban pointed out that Hungary's targeted growth rates double the EU's average for the next fifteen years, and that Hungary had a 5.9 percent unemployment rate in the first quarter of 2001, while the EU's average rate was 8 percent.

A Roma musician plays harmonica on the streets of Budapest. The Roma face severe discrimination in Hungary.

ETHNIC MINORITIES

In addition to immigration issues, the EU is also concerned with the way its members treat the ethnic minorities living within their borders. Hungary has a relatively small percentage (estimated at less than 10 percent) of non-Magyar people,

but there have been accusations of discrimination in employment and housing opportunities against these minorities.

Small groups of Germans, Slovaks, Croatians, Serbs, and Romanians live in Hungary, but the largest minority group is the Roma, who number between five hundred thousand and eight hundred thousand. The Roma are known worldwide as Gypsies, but the EU, the United Nations, and the ethnic group itself prefers the name Roma, which means "the people" in the Romany language they speak. Most of Hungary's Roma are poor, and they suffer from discrimination in the job market, housing, and social services. Unemployment among the Roma in Eastern Europe is estimated between 70 and 90 percent.

The EU, however, mandates that legislation guaranteeing equal treatment for all people, including the Roma, must be adopted and followed. "The goal of the European Union is that Roma citizens enjoy exactly the same political rights as any other citizen of the EU—no more, no less,"[25] said Ramirio Cibrian, head of the European Commission (the EU's executive body) delegation in Czechoslovakia.

To enforce these rules, the European Commission publishes a yearly report that examines the degree of compliance with the economic, social, and legal standards expected of EU members. A bad grade for human rights on this report can undo the positive image cast by years of economic reforms. Minority discrimination is one of the areas Hungary will have to improve in order to be accepted into the EU. The country has passed laws to make discrimination illegal, but on an individual level old habits are slow to change.

SPECIAL TREATMENT FOR HUNGARIAN NATIONALS

Another issue causing concern in the EU is a Hungarian law that went into effect January 1, 2002. This law grants ethnic Hungarians living in other countries special medical, employment, and education opportunities in Hungary.

There are approximately 5 million Magyars living outside the country's national borders. An estimated 2 million Hungarians who live in Transylvania (now a part of Romania) make up the largest ethnic minority in Europe. There are also large Hungarian populations in Slovakia (600,000), Yugoslavia and Croatia (650,000), Ukraine (200,000), and Austria (70,000). Another million Hungarians are scattered

WHO ARE THE ROMA?

The Roma, or Gypsies, consist of several distinct groups of Romany people who share a similar ethnic background but live in many countries around the world. Their language suggests that they migrated from the Indian subcontinent more than one thousand years ago.

Whatever their origin, the Roma wandered Europe for many generations without finding a homeland of their own. Their nomadic culture set them apart from the other people living around them, and they have often been viewed with suspicion and distrust. There are more than 12 million Roma in many countries. No one knows the exact number, however, because they are often not recorded on official census counts. Many Roma deliberately hide their ethnic background to protect themselves from prejudice and discrimination.

Many people associate the Roma with certain types of occupations, particularly fortune telling and musical entertainment. Although, historically, some Roma worked in these fields, they have also worked as mercenaries (paid soldiers), metalsmiths, basket makers, and servants. And today, even though more than 50 percent of Eastern Europe's Roma are unemployed, many have mainstream jobs, including carpentry and journalism, although some do still perform musical entertainment.

Gypsy musicians are often seen playing on the streets or in restaurants in Hungary. Gypsy music was originally performed a cappella (without instruments). But in Hungary, the musicians adapted to the demands of their audience and incorporated instruments and Hungarian folk music into their musical style. In addition to the street and restaurant musicians, Hungary also has several excellent Gypsy orchestras who perform in their home cities and produce records and tapes of their lively music.

throughout the United States, Canada, Australia, and Israel. Under the new law, these Hungarians could, without changing their residence, return to Hungary periodically for medical treatment, employment, or schooling.

Not everyone supports this measure, however. Neighboring countries—Slovakia and Romania in particular—opposed the law. They argued that the law will create tensions in their countries because native Slovakian and Romanian citizens will not have the same benefits as Hungarians. The EU has also spoken out against the law because the EU is against any regulation favoring one population over another.

Hungary's government refuses to abandon the law, hoping it will prevent mass migrations of ethnic Hungarians back into their homeland once the borders are open to immigration through EU membership. The Hungarians are working hard on compromises to overcome objections, however. Romania, for instance, withdrew its opposition after Hungary agreed to grant work permits to all Romanians, regardless of ethnicity. Romanian premier Adrian Nastase stated in a news conference, "We succeeded in . . . getting a compromise without letting this dispute contaminate a rather positive relationship."[26] Negotiations are still underway with Slovakia, and an agreement that satisfies all parties will likely satisfy the EU as well.

BRINGING AGRICULTURE UP TO PAR

Another area being given close attention by the EU is agriculture. The EU issues agriculture subsidies (financial support) to help member countries bring their production up to par. The agricultural systems of former Eastern bloc countries have declined since the fall of communism, however. This has caused some concern among EU members, who worry about how much it will cost to subsidize candidate nations.

Under the Communist system, Hungary's farmland was controlled by the state in large collective farms. Today, however, private owners and farming cooperatives work the land and have struggled to make the change to a market-oriented economy. It has not been easy. After the political and economic changes of 1989–1990, Hungary's agricultural output fell by 30 percent, and livestock production dropped by 50 percent. Farmers had to learn to manage their own land and production and to market their products. The process was made more difficult during the 1990s, because a series of floods and droughts in Hungary added to the farmers' burdens.

In spite of the problems, Hungary's government believes that the nation's agricultural system will be able to catch up to the Western European countries within a few years. A brochure published by Hungary's Ministry of Agriculture expresses confidence that Hungary will rise to the challenge and bring its agricultural sector up to EU standards. The brochure cites the country's excellent resources and history:

Hungarian agriculture goes back for more than one thousand years. Agricultural production was characterized even centuries ago by the fact that besides meeting domestic demands, Hungary exported considerable amounts. The most important agricultural products of our country, mainly cattle, wheat and wine, have been exported to the markets of Western and Northern Europe since the Middle Ages.

Approximately 70 percent of the area of Hungary is suitable for cultivation. The country's natural endowments, hours of sunshine, configurations of terrain and fertile soil, has meant good yields have been and still are being achieved. . . . Owing to favorable endowments, the quality of the country's fruits and vegetables are almost beyond compare.[27]

Despite this optimism, Hungary's current agricultural system has many problems, including low production and market development. Other candidate nations also have serious problems with their agricultural systems. For this reason, many current EU members worry that the candidate nations, if accepted for membership, would quickly drain the EU's budget for farm subsidies. It is true that, as of 2001, Hungary's farms are in need of subsidies. Yet over the past four years, Hungary has made progress toward bringing its agriculture up to European standards by improving its production, developing new markets, and experimenting with new products.

Despite such innovative measures, many Hungarian farmers are discouraged and would like to sell their farms and go into other kinds of work. The lack of local interest in farming has led to another problem. Some government officials worry that EU membership will bring an influx of foreign investors buying huge tracks of Hungarian land from the dissatisfied farmers. Presently, Hungarian law prohibits the sale of farmland to foreigners. However, many Austrian farmers have become absentee landowners through illegal private agreements with Hungarians. The Austrians hope to legalize their agreements when Hungary becomes a member of the EU. Prime Minister Orban is determined not to let this happen. He intends to reclaim these Hungarian farmlands in order to keep the land and the profits from it under Hungar-

BABY-FOOD BEEF

Several international baby food producers are interested in using Hungary's ancient breed of longhorn cattle in their baby-food beef. In the past several years, European cattle have suffered from outbreaks of two serious livestock diseases: mad cow disease and hoof-and-mouth disease. Both pose a serious threat to livestock, and a fatal form of mad cow disease can be transmitted to humans who eat infected beef.

The primitive Hungarian longhorn cattle have never been known to contract the disease, however. These cattle have roamed the *puszta* since before the Hungarian conquest in 896 and have never mixed or interbred with other cattle. Today they live primarily in Hungarian national parks. They eat only wild grass and herbs of the *puszta*. They are raised on the open range year-round and are given no supplementary feed. These conditions keep them free of mad cow disease. Therefore, Hungary has gained a new market for its native beef as baby food manufacturers seek to produce a safe, disease-free product.

ian control. Orban stated: "Austrians who circumvented the law can be happy to get away unpunished. We won't hurt them, their departure will suffice and we'll welcome them back as tourists."[28]

ENVIRONMENTAL ISSUES

A final issue of concern to the EU is the environment. Air and water quality problems, for instance, cannot be confined within the borders of polluting countries. Pollution spews out of a factory in one country and rides the air currents to spread across much of Europe. International waterways also carry pollutants downstream from the countries they pass through, and disruptions of the water flow affect countries both up- and downstream. Therefore, the environment is of vital interest to the EU, and strict controls are imposed on EU member countries.

Hungary has several environmental problems that require attention. Coal burning in homes and industry, for example, causes air pollution and acid rain. Waste such as buried toxic chemicals and jet fuel left by the Soviet military threaten the soil and groundwater supply. Hungary is working to meet EU

A fisherman collects dead fish from the Tisza River after a cyanide spill poisoned the water.

standards by cleaning up the pollutants and turning to cleaner fuel sources.

In addition to its own pollution problems, Hungary suffers from the environmental woes of its neighbors. In fact, some of the most serious environmental issues plaguing Hungary, such as problems involving the Danube River, are not of its own making. The Danube, one of Europe's most important rivers, travels through or forms borders for ten countries, and each downriver country suffers from upriver pollution. Hungary, for example, suffered serious environmental and economic damages in two recent cyanide spills. The first and most serious occurred in Romania and contaminated Hungarian sections of both the Tisza and Danube Rivers. Not only were fish and wildlife killed in staggering numbers, but the tourism industry in the area was almost wiped out. Only fifteen hundred tourists visited the region of Hungary around the Tisza last year, compared to a normal average of eighteen thousand to twenty thousand. In the spring of 2001, Hungary filed a $95 million lawsuit against Aurul, the Romanian chemical company accused of causing the spill.

Other times, upriver countries suffer from environmental events that occur downriver. For example, the Danube provides Hungary, a landlocked nation, access to the Black Sea. In 1999, in an attempt to force Yugoslavia to relinquish control of Kosovo, bombs dropped by the North Atlantic Treaty Organization (NATO) destroyed three bridges at the Serbian

NATO

In 1949, ten European and two North American nations signed the North Atlantic Treaty, creating an alliance committed to mutual defense from military enemies. Four more nations were admitted to the alliance between 1952 and 1982. On March 12, 1999, Hungary, the Czech Republic, and Poland joined the group now called the North Atlantic Treaty Organization (NATO), bringing the total number of member countries to nineteen.

The primary role of NATO is to provide a strong defense for member nations. The members are committed to building their defense capabilities and to participate in collective defense planning. Several articles of the treaty provide for specific situations. Article 5, for instance, states that an armed attack on any member of NATO will be deemed an attack against all members. In other articles, each member country agrees to contribute to building peaceful and friendly international relations, not only among member nations but also with nonmember nations.

Over the years, especially after the dramatic changes that occurred in Europe during the 1990s, NATO has adapted to meet the needs of the modern world. As a result, the organization's mission is no longer strictly military; it has accepted new roles in the fields of crisis management, peacekeeping, and peace support. One major part of these new functions involves reducing misunderstandings and mistrust among nations. In order to do this, NATO has formed partnerships with twenty-six non-NATO countries. This partnership program promotes cooperation in security-related activities among the NATO allies and the partner countries.

city of Sad. Tons of debris disrupted the flow of the river and blocked shipping. Hungary's vital shipping route to the Black Sea was cut off. Returning the river to its natural condition was of the utmost importance to Hungary and the other countries that depended on the Danube for shipping goods to and from Black Sea ports. In April 2001, a Danish-Hungarian company received a contract, funded by the EU, to clear the river of debris and restore shipping.

The issues standing between Hungary and EU membership are complex and often lead to heated debate. However, the EU and the candidate nations agree that expansion will eventually benefit everyone by forging a stronger Europe. And Hungary is proud to be in the forefront of the group of nations striving to meet EU qualifications.

HUNGARY'S CREATIVE SPIRIT

Through generations of foreign interference and domination, the Hungarian people have maintained a strong national and ethnic identity. The influence of different cultures has not overwhelmed the Hungarian identity. Instead, it has supplied the building blocks for a uniquely Hungarian creativity reflecting these many cultural influences. Hungarian creativity is sometimes political, sometimes strictly practical, and sometimes simply a celebration of love and beauty.

THE HEART OF A POET

Poetry has always been at the heart of Hungary's literary traditions. Hungary's poets have often been the first to voice discontent with political oppression and economic hardships. Journalist Yorick Blumenfeld writes, "Like the authors of the Bible, Hungarian poets are prophets among their people. The Hungarians believe poetry has the force, the vigor, to shape reality."[29] The acceptance of the poet as prophet, or as the voice of the people, is one reason that poetry is beloved by Hungarians of all ages and all walks of life. Through their writing, poets express the ideas and fears that much of the population feels but is afraid to voice. Blumenfeld continues:

> The readiness with which Hungarian poets have accepted involvement [in politics and society]—both romantic and political—certainly is one of the explanations for their phenomenal popularity. Over five hundred volumes of poetry a year were published in the mid-sixties [1960s].[30]

During the years of foreign control, Hungarian poets dared to defy their political oppressors by writing poetic political commentary. Both the Habsburgs and the Soviets tolerated political ideals expressed in poetry but silenced other voices of dissension. Revolutionary ideas expressed as poems

69

The nineteenth-century poet, Sandor Petofi is one of Hungary's most beloved literary figures.

seemed less threatening, the foreign powers reasoned. It was a policy that backfired. The poems actually motivated people to act. Hungary's poets have, therefore, been in the forefront of every major political movement in the country's history.

SANDOR PETOFI

One of Hungary's most beloved literary figures is the nineteenth-century poet, Sandor Petofi. Petofi not only produced brilliant lyrics, but he was also instrumental in producing two revolutions as well—one cost him his life, and the other occurred more than one hundred years after his death.

Petofi died in 1849 at the age of twenty-six on the battle-field of the unsuccessful revolution he helped start. His 1848 poem, "Rise Up Magyar," was a passionate plea to his compatriots to take up arms against the Austrians—it is now the national anthem of Hungary. The first verse of "Rise Up Magyar" expresses the poet's fervent patriotism:

Rise up, Magyar, the country calls!
It's "now or never" what fate befalls . . .
Shall we live as slaves or free men?
That's the question—choose your "Amen"
God of Hungarians, we swear unto thee,
We swear unto thee—that slaves we shall no longer be![31]

In 1956, almost one hundred years after Petofi's death, a new generation of poets and other writers, tired of the oppressive Soviet control, adopted his patriotic zeal and formed the Petofi Circle. This organization of writers and students voiced the nation's dissatisfaction with Soviet rule and sparked the Revolt of 1956. Poets were so influential in

A POET'S CRY OF FREEDOM

When the Hungarian revolt began on October 23, 1956, many Hungarian poets were inspired to express their feelings through poetry. The poem "The 23rd of October" was written by Tollas Tibor to commemorate the excitement and exhilaration of those few days before the Soviets crushed the revolution. Stephen Sisa included the poem, translated by Watson Kirkeonnel, in his book, *The Spirit of Hungary*.

The earth cries out in pain, the walls are falling
Blue trumpets to the sky with triumph smite
And from the dank stones of the dungeon crawling
Man issues forth again and walks in light.
Our withered bodies are a-flood with feeling.
Upon our faded cheeks the sunlight gleams.
Our steps are staggering, nay, almost reeling,
Our souls are bright with freedom and its dreams.
Our hearts, out of the dark, throw wide their portals
[doors],
A purple flower from the earth upsoars.
Out of our slavery, we show light to mortals,
Without a weapon, we are conquerors.

Hungary that during the revolt, newspapers printed poems by Petofi and others to emphasize the emotions that sparked the revolt. Noel Barber writes:

> Many papers printed poems on their front pages. Sandor Petofi's famous poem starting "the sea has risen, the sea of the people," appeared on no less than five broadsheets [newspapers] (on the same morning). Other papers printed new poems of varying quality "hammered out in the stress of the uprising."[32]

Even the Soviets ultimately recognized the importance of Hungary's poets. Remarking on the 1956 revolt, former Soviet premier Nikita Khrushchev stated, "If ten or so Hungarian writers had been shot at the right moment, the revolution would never have occurred."[33]

HUMOR: THE GREAT HEALER

Hungarians have a reputation for laughing in the face of misery, and, in the years after the failed 1956 revolt, their talent for biting satire came to full flower on the small stages of Budapest. Political satire, like poetry, was tolerated by the Communist regime because it was seen as a harmless expression of frustration and dissatisfaction. Communist leader Janos Kadar, who occasionally visited the Budapest theater called the Vidam Szinpad (Merry Stage), reportedly once said, "What the people laugh about on stage, they won't whisper behind closed doors."[34] Therefore, the government looked the other way as Hungarians found an outlet for their political frustrations by flocking to theaters to spend an evening laughing at themselves and their situation.

However, even in the open cabaret atmosphere of the theaters in the late 1950s and 1960s, certain topics were taboo—Jews, Czechs, Romanians, Gypsies, police officers, and current Communist leaders were not joking matters. Without offering reasons for what was not acceptable, the Communist Party dictated that these subjects be avoided. Hungarian humorists had to accept the restrictions or end their performances.

However, Hungarians could question political ideologies like communism and Marxism (the political system advocated by Karl Marx) even though their contemporary leaders were off limits. Istvan Fejer, until mid-1967 the director of the Merry Stage, presented a popular skit in which a drunken

RUBIK'S CUBE

Erno Rubik, a professor at the Academy of Applied Arts and Crafts in Budapest, had a passion for geometry, especially the study of three-dimensional forms. He was particularly interested in building small, complex structures. As an exercise in structural design, he wanted to produce a simple cube made up of smaller cubes, and he wanted to be able to move the blocks independently without the cube falling apart. He had no idea that this intellectual exercise would change his life.

As part of the process, Rubik put different-colored adhesive paper on each side of the cube. Then he twisted it. A March 1986 *Discover* magazine article reprinted on the PuzzleSolver website (puzzlesolver.com) quoted Rubik as saying that it was wonderful to watch the color parade, but when he decided to put the cubes back in order he faced an enormous challenge. Putting the cubes back in their original order was not easy. The cube has 43 quintillion wrong alignments, and only one correct one.

Despite those odds, Erno Rubik had created a new puzzle that became one of the most popular toys ever made. In 1974, Rubik patented his amazing cube in Hungary. Initially, a Hungarian company produced the cubes, but because of poor marketing, success was limited. Eventually, the British Ideal Toy Company bought 1 million cubes. With Ideal's international marketing, the first million sold quickly, and soon the cube spread around the world.

In spite of the cube's success, the Hungarian company that produced the first ones went out of business under the pressure keeping up with the demand for the new toy. The Communist system's economic plan was not designed to react quickly to market demands. The craze was over before the company could produce enough cubes to make a profit.

worker stops in a public park to speak at length to a statue of Karl Marx. In one scene, the drunk criticizes the Soviet political system, a system that made it almost impossible for ordinary Hungarian citizens to obtain luxury items like television sets and carpets. He admits to the Communist/Marxist concern that the more people have, the more they want. However, the drunk, speaking to the statue, explains that people also need incentive. He maintains that people can work toward personal rewards and still contribute to society. He says:

Erno Rubik's "cube" was immensely popular in America in the 1980's.

Everybody saves for something. . . . Ha, ha . . . then it comes: The socialist [Communist] house is a blessing: an apartment with parquet floors. A parquet floor needs a carpet. And where there is a carpet there must be a vacuum cleaner, and where there is a vacuum cleaner there must be a TV, and where there is a TV one should save for a car to get away from the TV—it is so terrible! Well, is this my fault Comrade Marx? I know, I know that one can work hard for mankind in a well-furnished house as well.[35]

PRESERVING TRADITION THROUGH ART AND MUSIC

Other venues of artistic expression have not been as outspoken politically as literature, but still carry a message of national pride. Hungary has produced many accomplished musicians, for instance. One of the most revered is pianist and composer Franz Liszt, who founded the Academy of Music in Budapest in 1875. Liszt, who claimed to be part Gypsy, is remembered for works such as his *Hungarian Rhapsodies*, which capture the fiery spirit of traditional Hungarian Gypsy music.

During the twentieth century, Bela Bartok and Zoltan Kodaly followed Liszt's example and built on the traditions of Hungarian folk music. The two composers traveled around the country collecting and recording thousands of Hungarian, Romanian, and Arabian folk songs. In doing so, they preserved the traditional music of the people, much of which had been passed from musician to musician but never captured on tape or paper. In addition, each of these composers blended elements of folk music he studied with modern influences to create his own compositions, such as Bartok's *Bluebeard's Castle* and Kodaly's *Peacock Variations*.

ARCHITECTURE: HARMONY AND DISCORD

Hungarian architecture is also a blend. Many foreign cultures left their mark on the architectural landscape of Hungary. Roman ruins can be seen on many sites throughout Hungary, and Pecs and Eger have fine examples of Turkish architecture. Catholic churches often feature elements of Byzantine architecture, and the Austrians left many examples of their ornamental baroque style, particularly in the northern counties.

Furthermore, single buildings often reflect more than one style. Many Hungarian buildings have been built, destroyed, and rebuilt since medieval times. Each renovation usually reflects the style of the time, so the various wings and architectural features of one building may include a variety of styles. Many of the buildings on Budapest's historic Castle Hill, for example, contain elements of several different styles. Sometimes these different styles blend into a pleasing whole, while other buildings appear to be constructed of unrelated parts.

The Hungarians celebrated their diverse architectural history with the creation of Vajdahunyad Castle. The castle, built as a nonpermanent display in Budapest's Varosliget Park for the 1896 millennial celebration, reflects the nation's history through a medley of architectural styles. The castle

Budapest's historic Castle Hill incorporates elements of many architectural styles.

includes reproductions of parts of several historical Hungarian buildings, including a Romanesque monastery. And the castle courtyard is presided over by a bronze statue of Anonymous, the medieval chronicler who first recorded Hungarian history. The amused Hungarians were delighted with the castle, and it was rebuilt after the millennium celebration to stand as a permanent reminder of one thousand years of conflict and rebuilding.

EDWARD TELLER'S CORVIN MEDAL

In August 2001, Dr. Edward Teller was honored with the Hungarian Corvin Medal, bestowed by the Hungarian government for exceptional achievement in the arts and sciences. The medal had not been awarded since 1930, and its first twenty-first-century recipient was one of the many Hungarians who contributed to science while living outside of Hungary.

Dr. Teller was awarded the medal primarily for his outstanding contributions in atomic and nuclear physics, but he was also cited at the presentation for his accomplishments as a poet and pianist. During the award presentation, several Hungarian diplomats spoke about Teller's contributions to Hungarian society. One of the speakers, Attila Varhegyi, a Hungarian diplomat, called Edward Teller a symbol for Hungary and the most distinguished Hungarian living in the world today. Another Hungarian diplomat, Maria Schmidt, delivered the message that Prime Minister Viktor Orban considered Teller's contributions toward ending the Cold War to be the primary force behind the fact that Hungary is again a free nation. By choosing, as a recipient of this award, a native Hungarian whose contributions took place outside of Hungary, the nation shows its pride in the many Hungarians who live and work outside the country's borders.

PRESERVING THE PAST THROUGH FOLK ART

In spite of the march of time and the growth of modern technology, Hungary has preserved its link to the past through rich folk art traditions that date back many generations. The folk art of Hungary is the work of ordinary people expressing the beauty of the world around them in a practical way. The Communist regime championed workers and, therefore revered folk art, the art of the common people. Consequently, during the Communist era, folk art lost favor with many sophisticated and politically conscious citizens who hated the Communist government. However, since the fall of communism, folk art has regained respect as an attractive decorative art as well as a reflection of ethnic heritage.

Hungarian folk artisans produce many wares, including useful household objects and clothing decorated with embroidery and painting. Clothing and table linens are adorned

*Embroidery is a
popular art form in
Hungary.*

with embroidery that ranges from delicate white-on-white
cutwork, to cheerful flowers standing bright against a white
background, to subtle earth tones on rough-woven fabrics.
The Paloc people of the northern uplands, especially around
the village of Holloko; the Matyo people of the northeastern
village of Mezokovesd; and the women of Kalocsa, a village
in the southern Great Plain, are particularly noted for their
fine embroidery that preserves old styles and traditions.

Hand-thrown pottery and delicately carved wooden objects are also popular. Jugs, pitchers, plates, bowls, cups, and inscribed wedding pots are often decorated with colorful painted figures and flowers. Less common, but equally popular, is the all-black pottery produced in the village of Nadudvar in the southern Great Plain. These glossy black bowls and vases are a rare and beautiful expression of the potter's art.

Hungarian craft shops, especially those in the Transdanubia region, sell carved and painted wooden and bone objects. These objects include everything from salt, pepper, and paprika containers to furniture and oak chests decorated with geometric shapes. Intricately carved puzzle boxes are particularly popular with tourists. The boxes consist of a series of cleverly concealed sliding panels that must be manipulated—first to expose a hidden key, then to uncover the keyhole to open the box, which often contains an additional hiding place behind a mirror or sliding panel.

A DRAIN ON CREATIVITY

Hungarian creativity has received global acclaim, especially as many talented artists, performers, and intellectuals now practice their trade outside of their native Hungary. Political, social, and economic conditions in Hungary have often forced the nation's brightest citizens to leave home, seeking a better life and the freedom to express their creativity. Of the historical events that caused a surge of Hungarians to leave the country, the most notable was the 1956 revolt, in which more than two hundred thousand Hungarians fled their homeland. The refugees included some of the most well-educated and most capable artists, scientists, engineers, and athletes. This loss of talent is often referred to as the brain drain.

Through war, revolution, and repression, Hungarians immigrated reluctantly, leaving behind homes and families but taking with them their education and intellect. Hungarian immigrants have made their homes in hundreds of countries around the world, and their contributions to their new homelands have been huge. Eight scientists of Hungarian birth were awarded Nobel prizes between 1914 and 1976; only one, Albert Szent-Gyorgyi, was working in Hungary when he received the prize.

Many Hungarian scientists were also involved in the United States's Manhattan Project to develop the atomic bomb, and later in the U.S. Atomic Energy Commission, the organization charged with controlling and developing the use of atomic energy. In fact, it was a Hungarian who suggested the project to President Roosevelt. According to Hungarian historian Zoltan Bodolai:

> The most eminent of these Hungarian-American scientists was Professor Leo Szilard, who demonstrated the possibility of atomic fission in 1939. With his friend, [Albert] Einstein, he suggested to President Roosevelt that he should set up an atomic research programme in the United States. The team of Szilard, [Edward] Teller, [Eugene] Wigner and [Janos Von] Neumann—all Hungarians —with the half-Hungarian Oppenheimer and the Italian Fermi constituted the successful Atomic Commission which eventually assured the United States the possession of the atomic bomb.[36]

Although the loss of creative talent and intellect has slowed to a trickle since the end of communism, it has not ended. Peter Makrai, a Hungarian software technician, calls the modern version "brain sucking,"[37] because affluent countries use money to draw the best talent away from Hungary. However, according to a newsletter published by the Embassy of Hungary in February 2001, the brain drain should soon be a thing of the past. The newsletter states that: "Analysts believe the brain drain will stop, partly because there are more research funds available domestically, and partly because an increasing number of multinationals are moving innovation centers to Hungary."[38] By moving some of their research and development centers to Hungary, large corporations are able to take advantage of the inventiveness of the Hungarians without uprooting them, and at the same time contribute to the country's economic growth. Hence as the brain drain ends, Hungary's contributions to the world society continue.

A WAY OF LIFE

6

A thousand years of being caught in the middle of the clash of East-West culture, ideology, and religion have forged the Hungarians into a unique people. Generations of domination by other nations served to build Hungarians' strength of character and their love of their Magyar heritage. They endured adversity but never bowed to it; instead they learned to face whatever life brought. Author Zoltan Bodolai writes:

> The Hungarians have never built pyramids, ruled slave empires, and conquered new worlds. They are a proud, strange, and lonely people. They live in the Carpathian basin and just about everywhere else, engaged in all possible (and some impossible) occupations. No two Hungarians are alike, and yet the magnetism of their diversity seems to bring them together: they seem to be united by their differences. When they meet, they greet each other like long lost brothers, laugh, dream and sing together for a while, then discover some of the innumerable, specially Hungarian differences and go their own, lonely ways, working and dreaming (they are very good at both) . . . .

> They believe in God. They also believe in miracles, in beautifully useless ideals, but first of all they have unlimited faith in themselves. They love women, music, poetry, romantic history (their own), pure mathematics, applied humor, sumptuous dresses, dignified or fiery dances, melancholic music—but most of all their unique language, a flowery relic of bygone ages with its strange mixture of oriental color and Nordic majesty.

> They have survived at the crossroads of history where more numerous nations had perished. Strangers came by the millions to join them and to die for them, attracted by that strange magic which is Hungary. They have survived and with them has survived a unique, complex culture, the synthesis of ancient Euro-Asian humanism and modern, western Christianity.[39]

81

DIFFERING VIEWPOINTS

Part of the Hungarian character is reflected in a love of debating differing opinions, and issues are often hotly debated among friends and families. Politics and the changes that have occurred since 1989 are favorite topics. More than ten years after the fall of communism, Hungarians still have mixed feelings about the change to capitalism. Perceptions vary widely and are often shaped by age and social or economic position. Some, especially older people, miss the security offered by communism. Others revel in the personal freedoms and the new opportunities offered by the new system.

Imre Makrai and his family highlight some of those differences of opinion. The Makrais are well-educated middle-class citizens of Budapest. Imre is a retired teacher and his wife Judit is semiretired from the same profession. Their twenty-five-year-old son, Peter, works for a large international electronics firm.

Imre Makrai believes that for most Hungarians, "the change in 1989 did not bring the wished system."[40] He explains that the Communist Party ideology has been replaced by a system based on money, and the value of Hungarian money has deteriorated. Not only does money buy less now than it did under communism, but also the state has moved away from social support in areas such as health care, subsidized holidays, and education. All of these things were much

PUTTING FIRST NAMES LAST

In Hungary, last, or family, names always come before first, or given, names—a practice that is unusual outside of Asia. For example, Janos Kovacs (Hungarian for John Smith) would be called Kovacs Janos. Titles like *Mr.* (*ur.* in Hungarian) also follow the name, so Mr. John Smith would be Kovacs Janos ur. Married women also use titles that follow their name, so Mrs. John Smith would be called Kovacs Janosne, with the *ne* added to indicate her married status.

However, many modern women choose a more personalized system, retaining their original first and last name as part of their married name. If Szabo Zsuzsi (Hungarian for Susan Taylor) married John Smith, for instance, she could also be known as Susan Taylor Smith, or Kovacsne Szabo Zsuzsi in Hungarian.

A middle-class family in Budapest spends a Sunday afternoon ice skating.

less expensive under communism. In those days, with so many things subsidized by the government, most people could easily afford entertainment such as dining out, theater, and cinema. Today, Imre says, most Hungarians cannot afford those luxuries, and the primary entertainment is watching TV. Imre says that it is frustrating to many Hungarians to see the affluence of the West on TV when they cannot attain a similar standard of living for themselves.

Imre does, however, recognize that some consumer goods that were unavailable only a few years ago appear in many Hungarian homes today. His wife agrees, saying, "If you have money now, you can find everything in the shops."[41] Almost every family has a TV, refrigerator, and washing machine; many have microwaves, electric mixers, and VCRs. Cell phones are particularly popular with young people; in 2001 the number of cell phones in Hungary topped 3 million. Yet according to Imre Makrai, an average Hungarian family has very little to spend on such consumer goods. Rent and utilities take approximately half of the average family's salary, and since the fall of communism, the range of income between average Hungarians and the nation's elite has grown considerably. Imre Makrai says, "The representatives [members of the government] and the savvy entrepreneurs' salary is getting close to Western European standards, while the other half of the population vegetates on Eastern European salaries."[42]

As a teacher, Judit Baldy Makraine (the *ne* added to her name indicates her married status) laments the fact that teachers' salaries have not kept up with technical and marketing fields, which have increased by approximately 17 percent as compared to 7 percent for teachers. She believes that it is very important for teachers to receive good salaries because good teachers produce well-educated, skilled citizens. Yet with the current low salaries in the teaching field, commercial enterprises can draw the best teachers away from education by offering them much higher incomes.

The Makrais' son, Peter, often does not share his parents' opinions. Instead he views the changes brought by capitalism with optimism. Peter says:

> It is true that the average worker had a much better life [under communism] in terms of money, but we know that all the things were so cheap in communism because the country was making bigger and bigger debts and now we have to pay the price. That kind of economy wouldn't have been able to go on forever. [Now] I see that the Hungarian economy is going towards the right direction.
>
> It is interesting that in this new generation, all the young people are working in the commercial and technical fields and make much higher salaries than people now at middle age. So young people are actually spending a lot of money for all kinds of consumer stuff,

and they go out to restaurants and so on. It is a big change.

What I don't like [about capitalism] is the consumer society, but I guess that just comes with democracy. And with it came more crime and graffiti on the walls and so on. While under communism, there were no Mc-Donalds or big Western-style shopping malls, now those are here in full scale. I don't like though, the big Americanism, for example 80 percent of the movies on TV are American—but that is also true in Western European countries.[43]

Considering both positive and negative changes since the end of communism, Peter Makrai believes that, in spite of the increased crime rate and inflation, the overall effect is for the better, especially for his generation. He especially enjoys the freedom of movement; travel to noncommunist countries was forbidden under Soviet rule. Peter says: "Now we can travel freely in the world wherever we want. In the past, you were not allowed to leave the Eastern bloc. We young people can't even really imagine how it was in the past because we just hop on an airplane and go to Sweden or wherever."[44]

MODERN LIFESTYLES

Like the Makrais, most modern Hungarians live in city apartments or small suburban or rural houses. Some apartment dwellers have spacious rooms in pre–World War II homes that have been converted to apartments. Many Hungarians, however, live in drab, boxlike apartment complexes built under communism to ease the severe post-World War II housing shortage. Because of the high cost and limited availability of housing in Hungary, it is common for young adults to live with their parents; sometimes three generations share the family home. However, during the 1990s, housing construction increased, and because many young people are now making higher salaries, some have the option of having their own apartment.

Whatever the style of their home, Hungarians use family pictures, prized possessions, and window boxes of cheery flowers to bring warmth and charm to their home. Hungarians, who live in single-family homes often have gardens overflowing with flowers and herbs, and many city families also have garden plots outside of the city where they grow vegetables and fruit.

Many Hungarian families also own automobiles and enjoy the freedom and ease of travel in their own vehicle. However, because the price of gasoline is high, people often prefer public transportation or bicycles for daily transportation; in rural areas, horse-drawn wagons are common. Cities have excellent public transportation systems, and fast, efficient train travel is available between major cities. A network of bus routes ties rural areas together.

The trolley system in Budapest offers excellent public transportation.

Superhighways are limited in Hungary, but secondary roads are generally good and traffic is not usually excessive. Public transportation and the relatively good road system make travel within the country easy and allow for efficient transport of goods, such as the fruit and vegetables Hungary is known for producing. Today these products are shipped all over the country to be available to consumers wherever they live.

HUNGARIAN CUISINE

The food of Hungary developed from nomadic Asian traditions and evolved through succeeding waves of invaders. The result is an exotic, tasty, and spicy cuisine that reflects both Eastern and Western influences. The Romans, who arrived around the first century, began a tradition of growing grapes, grains, and fruit trees, while the Magyars contributed a simple diet based on meat and milk products. The Roman and Magyar diets gradually combined to produce a cuisine known for rich and spicy sauces, stews, and sweets.

The Hungarians still use milk products, especially sour cream, liberally and enjoy meats grilled simply on an open fire or simmered in rich stews. The best-known Hungarian stew is goulash, which means "herdsman's stew." Over the years goulash evolved from a simple Magyar shepherd's meal to a rich paprika-flavored stew with as many variations as there are cooks.

Paprika not only flavors goulash, but has become the signature seasoning of Hungarian food. The flavors of meats and vegetables of all kinds are combined with sour cream and generously seasoned with paprika.

In addition to milk and meat, the Magyar contributed *tarhonya*, tiny pellet-shaped noodles. Under the influence of Hungary's European neighbors, the Austrians, these simple noodles evolved into a wide range of grain products including dumplings, rich pastries, and breads.

During their 150-year occupation of the country, the Turks also influenced Hungarian cuisine. Under the Turks, Hungarians developed a taste for coffee and the paper-thin leaves of dough that the Turks use for baklava. Ultimately, these sheets of dough became the basis for Hungarian fruit strudels. Strudels and other delicious Hungarian pastries and cakes are available at bakeries and coffee shops all over

Grapes grown in Southern Transdanubia produce Hungary's finest red wines.

the country. Many homemakers also enjoy baking their own pastries, especially for holidays.

In addition to food, drink is also an important part of Hungarian cuisine. Hungary has produced excellent wines and fruit brandies for many hundreds of years. Hungary's finest red wines are produced in southern Transdanubia, and the best white wines come from the Lake Balaton area. However, the red wines of Eger and the sweet white wine of the Tokaj region are the best known outside of the country. Among brandies, apricot is by far the most popular, but brandies made from plums, pears, and peaches are also enjoyed.

Although these beverages are also a significant export product, they remain an important part of dining and celebrations inside the country as well. Alcohol consumption in Hungary is high. According to a world alcohol consumption report posted on the Internet, in 1999 Hungary, with 9.7 liters of pure alcohol consumed per capita, ranked ninth in the world for per capita alcohol consumption.

LOOKING TO A HIGHER POWER

Hungarians have always been somewhat skeptical of rigid religious doctrine. This may be because the country has been awash with changing religious influences for more than a thousand years. Accordingly, the people have become tolerant of different theologies. King Stephen made it clear to his subjects that adopting Christianity was the safest religious choice for eleventh-century Hungary—regardless of what one's underlying beliefs might be. By the time of the Protestant Reformation, Stephen's influence had waned, and the majority of Hungarians became Protestants. Many of those reverted to Catholicism during the Counter Reformation under the Habsburgs, although modern Hungary still has a sizeable Protestant population. Further, during the Turkish

PAPRIKA

Fiery red paprika is an important ingredient in many Hungarian dishes—especially those such as goulash that have become internationally popular. Paprika peppers are grown primarily in the area around Szeged and Kalocsa, in the southwestern part of the Great Plain. In fact, Kalocsa, known for the bright red peppers that hang in long strings to dry on the eaves of its traditional wooden houses, is called the paprika capital. About 10,000 tons of the spice are produced there annually, 55 percent of which is exported.

No one knows for sure how paprika got to Hungary. It may have originated in India and been brought to Hungary by the Turks, or it may have come from the New World, where many types of pepper were cultivated. Whatever its origin, paprika has been cultivated on the edge of the Great Plain since the sixteenth century. There are many varieties of paprika available fresh and dried in Hungary, but the ground spice, usually classified as "hot" or "sweet," is the most common form exported to international markets.

Not only is paprika a delicious seasoning, but it is also richer in vitamin C than citrus fruits. In fact, Hungarian scientist Dr. Albert Szent-Gyorgyi of Szeged, who worked with the paprika pepper, was awarded the Nobel prize for medicine in 1937 for being the first to isolate vitamin C. Hungarians, however, value their peppers for the rich, spicy flavor and consider the healthy vitamin C content just an added benefit.

occupation, many Hungarians converted to Islam—though not always by choice.

After World War II, the Communist Party wanted people to be guided by the state—not religion—and therefore saw Hungary's churches more as enemies than allies. As a result, Communist officials dismissed or arrested many of the priests and high church officials and replaced them with Communist sympathizers. Having familiar religious leaders replaced with Communist Party members created feelings of mistrust between parishioners and clergy, and many people turned away from church. Since the fall of communism, though, this attitude has gradually changed, and there has been some renewal of church participation. Peter Makrai says, "More people go to churches nowadays after the '89 change, compared to the past when assigned party members were monitoring and keeping records of people who went to churches."[45]

Today, even if they do not attend church, most Hungarians profess an affiliation to some religious organization. About 68 percent of those declaring a religious affiliation say they are Roman Catholic, 21 percent Reformed (Calvinist) Protestant, and 6 percent Evangelical (Lutheran) Protestant. There are also several smaller denominations. Judaism, for instance, has seen a revival since the end of communism. Today, there are approximately eighty thousand Jews living in Hungary. In spite of the revival of religion as an important part of life, churches and synagogues are seldom filled to capacity.

ON THE PLAYING FIELD

Sports arenas, however, are often full. Hungarians, as players and spectators, are enthusiastic about sports and competitions of all kinds. They excel at games that call for both mental and physical abilities.

Hungarians have always been among the masters at chess, for example. And three Hungarian women players in particular —Judit, Zsuzsi, and Sophia Polgar—stand out. In 1988 the three sisters, aged twelve, fourteen, and nineteen respectively, defeated the Soviet Union women's team. Zsuzsi Polgar, the middle sister, was recognized as a prodigy at the age of four when she won ten games out of ten at the Budapest chess championship for children under eleven. By the age of fifteen she was the number two women's player in the world—

topped only by her younger sister Judit. In 2001 Zsuzsi earned the title of Chess Champion of the World for women.

In more physical pastimes, soccer is a national favorite. Fall brings cheering Hungarians to the soccer field, whether they watch their local team compete against another Hungarian team or the national team battle it out in an international competition. Between 1950 and 1954, the Hungarian National Soccer Team achieved legendary fame by remaining undefeated. And the soccer team has brought home the Olympic gold three times, in 1952, 1964, and 1968.

Overall, Hungary has won 331 Olympic medals spanning a wide range of sports. In addition to soccer, Hungary has been particularly strong in fencing, the modern pentathlon, and gymnastics. Hungary's greatest overall Olympic triumph came in Helsinki, Finland, in 1952, when it won sixteen gold, ten silver, and seventeen bronze medals to take third place; only the United States and the Soviet Union won more medals.

However, Hungary's most memorable win came in the next round of Olympic games held in 1956 in Melbourne, Australia. Hungarian writer Stephen Sisa writes:

> In the gloriously tragic year of 1956, with the wounds of Russia's crushing defeat of the Revolution still fresh, Hungary managed to win nine gold, ten silver and eight bronze medals, finishing fourth in over-all Olympic standing behind only the United States, the Soviet Union and Germany. The most dramatic event of those games, which that year were held in Melbourne, was the water polo final in which Hungary faced the Soviet Union. The battle, fought both above the water and under it, was so brutal that the pool turned red from the blood of the injuries the players inflicted upon each other—but the score was wildly cheered by the millions who viewed the event either in the stands or on global television: Hungary 5, the Soviet Union 2. No victory was welcomed by the free world with more enthusiasm than this one.[46]

LOVE OF THE LAND

The Hungarians' enthusiasm for sports extends to outdoor nature sports as well. Activities like hunting and fishing are popular, and Hungarians enjoy the natural beauty of their country.

A Hungarian farmer poses with his workhorse. Hungarians enjoy the great outdoors and work hard to preserve their land.

Their love of the land has prompted them to take care to preserve it. Hungary's protected land areas constitute 67,060,000 acres, or 7.6 percent of the country's total area. The protected land falls into several categories; 2,620,000 acres have been declared national conservation land areas, and regional conservation land areas top 46,660,000 acres. Nine national parks make up the rest.

These protected areas help preserve Hungary's unique plant and wildlife populations. Hungary has more than two thousand flowering plant species. The country is also home to many common European wildlife species, and a few rare ones such as the wildcat and lake bat.

Three-fourths of Hungary's 450 vertebrates are birds. Abundant water supplies and extensive marshes make Hungary especially attractive to waterfowl. Of Europe's estimated 395 species of birds, 373 have been seen in Hungary.

Hungary's nine national parks also offer protection to some of the nation's most environmentally sensitive lands.

Hortogaby National Park near Debrecen is the largest, with 6,300,000 acres. This park protects the wildlife, fragile wetlands and marsh, and saline grasslands of the *puszta*, and it provides grazing land for the native gray Hungarian cattle and *racka* sheep. Parks such as the Bukk and Aggtelek National parks protect the northern woodlands and the system of karst (porous limestone) caves and streams of the region, while others protect lakes and rivers.

Hungarians also preserve their country's history in parks and living history museums. In villages such as Holloko in the northern uplands, visitors can see villagers living as they did generations ago. The people of the village wear traditional costumes and use the tools and household implements of their ancestors. Another example is the memorial park at Opusztaszer, where a panoramic painting and exhibits of artifacts and photographs trace the history of the Magyar from their first arrival in Hungary.

The Hungarians clearly take great pride in their land, wildlife, history, language, competitions, and lifestyle. They have also been shaped by their past. Their national anthem calls Hungarians "a people torn by fate." The burdens of their fate have made them reserved and formal people who retain a streak of romanticism and a love of beauty. Bodalai writes of his people: "There are about 15 million Hungarians in the world today: not quite 0.5 percent of mankind. Without them the sun would still rise and life would still go on—but the rainbow would be a little paler, music a little duller, women a little sadder and mankind a little poorer."[47]

FACTS ABOUT HUNGARY

GOVERNMENT

Full name: Republic of Hungary

Type: Parliamentary democracy

Head of state: President Arpad Goncz since 1990

Head of government: Prime Minister Viktor Orban since 1998

National flag: Tricolor of horizontal red, white, and green bands

Capital: Budapest

Administrative divisions: 19 counties and Budapest

GEOGRAPHY

Area: 37,212 square miles (1 percent of the area of Europe), of which 36,936 square miles is land and 276 square miles is water

Coastline: none (landlocked)

Location: East-central Europe (borders with Austria, Slovakia, Ukraine, Romania, Serbia, Croatia, Slovenia)

State border length: 897 miles

Highest peak: Mount Kekes (1014m) in the Matra Mountains

Longest rivers: The Danube extends through Hungary 167 miles; tributaries include the Szamos, Kraszna, Koros, Maros, Hernad, Sajo, and Berettyo Rivers

Largest lakes: Balaton (240 square mile surface area); Velence Lake (10 square mile surface area); Ferto Lake (129 square mile surface area; Hungarian part 33 square mile)

Climate: Temperate: cold, cloudy, humid winters; warm summers. Average temperatures: January, 28 degrees Fahrenheit; July, 73 degrees Fahrenheit

PEOPLE

Population: 10,3000,000 (21 percent under 14 years of age and 60 percent between 15 and 59 years of age)

Overall population density: 110 (per square km)

Distribution: 60 percent urban; 40 percent rural

Population growth rate (2000): -0.33 percent

Birth rate (2000): 9.26 births per 1,000 population

Death rate (2000): 13.34 deaths per 1,000 population

Life expectancy (1980): male, 66 years; female, 74 years (decreasing)

Literacy (1980): 99 percent of the population age 15 and over can read and write—99 percent of males and 98 percent of females

Ethnic groups: Hungarian, 89.9 percent; Roma, 4 percent; German, 2.6 percent; Serb, 2 percent; Slovak, 0.8 percent; Romanian, 0.7 percent

Major cities (1995): Budapest (2 million), Debrecen (210,000), Miskolc (182,000), Szeged (177,000), Gyor (127,000), Pecs (163,000)

Language: Hungarian

Major Religions: Roman Catholic (majority), Protestant, Jewish

ECONOMY

Monetary unit: Hungarian forint (HUF)

Natural resources: bauxite, coal, natural gas, fertile soils, arable land

Land use: Arable land, 51 percent; permanent crops, 3.6 percent; permanent pastures, 12.4 percent; forests and woodland, 19 percent; other, 14 percent

NOTES

INTRODUCTION: WHERE EAST MEETS WEST

1. Rudyard Kipling, *The Works of Rudyard Kipling*. Roslyn, New York: Black's Readers Service, pg. 53.

2. C.A. Macartney, *Hungary: A Short History*. Don Mabry's Historical Text Archive, chapter 1, p. 1. www.fortunecity.com.

3. Embassy of the Republic of Hungary in Zagreb, "The Path from the Orient to Our Present Homeland: The Birth and Achievements of Hungarian Oriental Studies," www.hungemb.hr.

4. Stephen Sisa, *The Spirit of Hungary*. Corvinus Library. www.hungary.com.

CHAPTER 2: THE MAGYARS: TUGGED BETWEEN EAST AND WEST

5. Istvan Lazar, *Hungary: A Brief History*. Budapest: Corvina Books, 1989, p. 7.

6. Macartney, *Hungary: A Short History*, chapter 1, p. 8.

7. Macartney, *Hungary: A Short History*, chapter 1, p. 6.

8. Macartney, *Hungary: A Short History*, chapter 1, p. 6.

9. Macartney, *Hungary: A Short History*, chapter 2, p. 2.

10. Quoted in Peter F. Sugar, ed., *A History of Hungary*. Bloomington: Indiana University Press, 1990, p. 27.

11. Quoted in Sugar, *A History of Hungary*, p. 70.

CHAPTER 3: THE UNCONQUERABLE SOUL OF HUNGARY

12. Quoted in Sugar, *A History of Hungary*, p. 295.

13. Stephen R. Burant, ed., *Hungary: A Country Study*, 2d ed. Washington, DC: Library of Congress, 1990, p. 43.

14. Endre Marton, *The Forbidden Sky*. Boston: Little, Brown, 1971, p. 101.

15. Noel Barber, *Seven Days of Freedom: The Hungarian Uprising, 1956*. New York: Stein and Day, 1974, p. 22.

16. Quoted in Sugar, *A History of Hungary*, p. 383.

17. Quoted in James A. Michener, *The Bridge at Andau.* New York: Random House, 1957, pp. 202–204.

18. Barber, *Seven Days of Freedom*, p. 232.

19. Macartney, *Hungary: A Short History*, chapter 10, p. 4.

20. Robert O. Paxton, *Europe in the Twentieth Century.* San Diego: Harcourt Brace Jovanovich, 1991, p. 670.

Chapter 4: From Communism to the European Union

21. Janos Dobszay, "The Churches, Religion, and Politics After 1989," *Hungarian Quarterly*, Winter 1996, www.net.hu.

22. *The Hungarian Government: Following the 1998 Parliamentary Elections.* Budapest: The Hungarian Ministry of Foreign Affairs, September 1998.

23. Gyorgy Csepeli, "Transition Blues: The Roots of Pessimism," *Hungarian Quarterly*, Summer 2000. www.hungeco.com.

24. Quoted in Gabor Turi, ed., *Entrepreneurial Spirit and Perseverance.* Embassy of Hungary, February 2001. www.hungaryemb.org.

25. Quoted in Eva Munk, "East Europe's Gypsies See EU Silver Lining," AOL News, June 5, 2001.

26. Quoted in Emese Bartha, "Hungary, Romania Sign Key Pact on Minority Law," AOL News, December 22, 2001.

27. *The Hungarian Agriculture and Food Industry in Figures.* Ministry of Agriculture and Regional Development. www.gak.hu.

28. Quoted in "Hungary Reclaimimg Disputed Land," AOL News, July 19, 2001.

Chapter 5: Hungary's Creative Spirit

29. Yorick Blumenfeld, *Seesaw: Cultural Life in Eastern Europe.* New York: Harcourt, Brace and World, 1968, p. 138.

30. Blumenfeld, *Seesaw*, p. 139.

31. "National Song," My Favorite Poems by Sandor Petofi, www.rci.rutgers.edu.

32. Barber, *Seven Days of Freedom*, p. 102.

33. Quoted in Barber, *Seven Days of Freedom*, p. 17.

34. Quoted in Blumenfeld, *Seesaw*, p. 79.

35. Quoted in Blumenfeld, *Seesaw*, p. 82.

36. Zoltan Bodolai, *The Timeless Nation: The History, Literature, Music, Art, and Folklore of the Hungarian Nation.* Corvinus Library, chapter 30. www.hungary.com.

37. Peter Makrai, interview by author, e-mail, May 21, 2001.

38. Gabor Turi, ed., *Brain Drain Is About to Stop.* Embassy of Hungary, February 2001. www.hungaryemb.org.

CHAPTER 6: A WAY OF LIFE

39. Bodolai, *The Timeless Nation*, chapter 2.

40. Imre Makrai, interview by author, e-mail, May 21, 2001.

41. Judit Baldy Makraine, interview by author, e-mail, May 21, 2001.

42. Imre Makrai, interview.

43. Peter Makrai, interview.

44. Peter Makrai, interview.

45. Peter Makrai, interview.

46. Sisa, *The Spirit of Hungary*.

47. Bodolai, *The Timeless Nation*, chapter 30.

CHRONOLOGY

896
Under the leadership of Arpad, the seven Hungarian tribes settle in the Carpathian basin.

997–1038
The reign of Stephen, son of Geza.

1000
Stephen named king by the pope. After his death, Stephen was canonized.

1241
The Mongolian Tatars devastate the country. Though only present one year, they halted development for at least a century.

1458–1490
The reign of King Matthias.

1526
At Mohacs, the present southern frontier of the country, the Turks defeat the Hungarian army. One hundred fifty years of Turkish occupation begins.

1541
The Turks occupy Buda. Hungary is split into three parts, with the western part of the country governed by the Habsburgs, the central area by the Turks, and the southeastern Transylvanian principality by a Hungarian.

1686
Buda recaptured from the Turks.

1848–1849
Revolution against the Habsburgs. With help from the Russian army, the Habsburgs win.

1867
The Hungarians conclude a compromise with the Austrians, and the Austro-Hungarian Dual Monarchy is established.

1873
Pest, Buda, and Obuda are unified. The first underground railway in continental Europe is put into operation in Budapest.

1914
World War I begins. Hungary as part of the Dual Monarchy enters the war with the Austrians.

1918
World War II ends, ending the Austro-Hungarian Dual Monarchy.

1920
The Trianon treaty reduces Hungary's area by two-thirds and the population by one-third.

1939
World War II begins. Hungary, in hopes of regaining lost territory, enters the war on the side of the Germans.

1944
The Nazis occupy Hungary, as they do not consider it a reliable ally.

1945
The Soviet Army liberates and occupies Hungary.

1956
A revolution against communism is defeated by Soviet troops.

1989–1990
The Communist Party voluntarily gives up its autocracy. A multiparty parliamentary democracy comes into being in Hungary. The Soviet army leaves Hungary.

1999
Hungary becomes a full member of NATO.

SUGGESTIONS FOR FURTHER READING

BOOKS

Anne Ake, *Austria*. San Diego, CA: Lucent Books, 2001. An overview of Austria and the Austro-Hungarian Empire.

Michael G. Kort, *The Handbook of the New Eastern Europe*. Brookfield, CT: Twenty-First Century Books, 2001. Up-to-date overview of the history and current affairs of Eastern Europe through the year 2000.

PERIODICALS

Jon Thompson, "East Europe's Dark Dawn: The Iron Curtain Rises to Reveal a Land Tarnished by Pollution," *National Geographic*, June 1991.

WEBSITES

Covinus Library, 1996–1999, Hungary. (www.hungary.com). An excellent collection of on-line English language books, articles, and Internet links about Hungary.

Hungary Network (www.hu.net). This website publishes the *Hungarian Quarterly*, an English-language journal of Hungarian arts and society. With back issues carried on-line for several years, this journal includes fiction, poetry, book reviews, exclusive interviews, important documents, background information, and essays on archaeology, music, the fine arts, theater, and film.

The Hungary Page (www.hungary.org). This multipage site contains useful information on Hungary, both historical and current.

Peter Makrai's Website (www.geocities.com/TheTropics/Shores/8520/hungary3.htm). This website contains the author's account of a visit to Transylvania, formerly part of Hungary and still home to a large Hungarian ethnic population. It also contains links to other informative Hungarian websites as well as photos of Budapest and other parts of Hungary.

PuzzleSolver (www.puzzlesolver.com). This website provides solutions to numerous puzzles, including Rubik's Cube.

WORKS CONSULTED

BOOKS

Noel Barber, *Seven Days of Freedom: The Hungarian Uprising, 1956.* New York: Stein and Day, 1974. Foreign correspondent Barber's firsthand story of the 1956 revolt is gripping. Barber was shot in the head during the revolt.

Yorick Blumenfeld, *Seesaw: Cultural Life in Eastern Europe.* New York: Harcourt, Brace and World, 1968. An in-depth study of culture in Eastern Europe during the Communist years.

Stephen R. Burant, ed., *Hungary: A Country Study.* 2nd ed. Washington, DC: Library of Congress, 1990. A well-researched and informative overview of Hungary up to the end of the Soviet era.

Rudyard Kipling, *The Works of Rudyard Kipling.* Roslyn, New York: Black's Readers Service. The collected works of Rudyard Kipling are presented in this volume.

Sandor Kopacsi, *In the Name of the Working Class: The Inside Story of the Hungarian Revolution.* New York: Grove Press, 1986. A personal account of the revolution by a former Budapest chief of police.

Istvan Lazar, *Hungary: A Brief History.* Budapest: Corvina Books, 1989. A colorful and entertaining history of Hungary.

Endre Marton, *The Forbidden Sky.* Boston: Little, Brown, 1971. A first-person story of the Revolt of 1956. Endre Marton, a graduate of Budapest University, won numerous awards for his news coverage of Budapest from 1947 to 1957. His journalism also won him eighteen months in an AVO prison before the revolution.

James A. Michener, *The Bridge at Andau.* New York: Random House, 1957. Michener uses the storytelling skills that brought him fame as a novelist to bring life to this nonfiction account of the people and events he encountered at this historic bridge—the primary escape point for the two hundred thousand Hungarian citizens who fled after the 1956 revolution.

Robert O. Paxton, *Europe in the Twentieth Century.* San Diego: Harcourt Brace Jovanovich, 1991. A comprehensive look at the major events in Europe during the twentieth century.

David Pryce-Jones, *The Hungarian Revolution.* New York: Horizon Press, 1969. This well-written book on the Hungarian revolution is illustrated with many photographs.

Peter F. Sugar, ed., *A History of Hungary.* Bloomington: Indiana University Press, 1990. An authoritative history of Hungary through the end of the Communist era, written by a number of distinguished contributors.

PERIODICALS AND FACT SHEETS

Peter Godwin, "Gypsies: The Outsiders," *National Geographic*, April 2001.

The Hungarian Education System. Budapest: The Hungarian Ministry of Foreign Affairs, 1996.

The Hungarian Government: Following the 1998 Parliamentary Elections. Budapest: The Hungarian Ministry of Foreign Affairs, September 1998.

INTERNET SOURCES

Emese Bartha, "Hungary, Romania Sign Key Pact on Minority Law," AOL News, December 22, 2001.

Zoltan Bodolai, *The Timeless Nation: The History, Literature, Music, Art, and Folklore of the Hungarian Nation.* Corvinus Library. www.hungary.com.

Gyorgy Csepeli, "Transition Blues: The Roots of Pessimism," *Hungarian Quarterly*, Summer 2000. www.hungeco.com.

"Cyanide Spill Leads to Severe Economic Loss—Study," AOL News, May 18, 2001.

Janos Dobszay, "The Churches, Religion, and Politics After 1989," *Hungarian Quarterly*, Winter 1996.

"Dr. Edward Teller Honored with Revived Hungarian Corvin Medal," AOL News, August 20, 2001.

Embassy of the Republic of Hungary in Zagreb, "The Path from the Orient to Our Present Homeland: The Birth and Achievements of Hungarian Oriental States." www.hungemb.hr.

"EU Candidates Call for Clear Farm Policy," AOL News, April 30, 2001.

"EU Gives Farming a Tough Row to Hoe," *Budapest Sun Online*, January 28, 1999. www.budapestsun.com.

The Hungarian Agriculture and Food Industry in Figures. Ministry of Agriculture and Regional Development. www.gak.hu.

"Hungarian Economy," *Encyclopedia of Hungarian Economy '99.* www.hungeco.com.

"Hungary Reclaiming Disputed Land," AOL News, July 19, 2001.

"Hungary/Slovak PMs Denounce EU Labour Restriction," AOL News, April 23, 2001.

Tamas S. Kiss, "BSE-Free Cattle in EU Spotlight," *Budapest Sun Online*, February 8, 2001. www.budapestsun.com.

Jonathon Lynn, "EU Enlargement Tops Agenda as Ministers Open Talks," AOL News, May 5, 2001.

C.A. Macartney, *Hungary: A Short History.* Don Mabry's Historical Text Archive, chapter 1, p. 1. www.fortunecity.com.

Eva Munk, "East Europe's Gypsies See EU Silver Lining," AOL News, June 5, 2001.

"National Song," My Favorite Poems by Sandor Petofi. www.rci.rutgers.edu.

Sandor Peto, "Hungary Seen as East Europe Labour Hub—Premier," AOL News, May 31, 2001.

Kristen Schweizer, "Hungary Defends Status Law, Says Eases Tensions," AOL News, May 24, 2001.

————, "Labour Concerns Haunt Hungary Ahead of EU Summit," AOL News, May 25, 2001.

Stephen Sisa, *The Spirit of Hungary*. Corvinus Library. www.hungary.com.

Gabor Turi, ed., *Brain Drain Is About to Stop*. Embassy of Hungary, February 2001. www.hungaryemb.org.

————, *Entrepreneurial Spirit and Perseverance*. Embassy of Hungary, February 2001. www.hungaryemb.org.

INDEX

PICTURE CREDITS

ABOUT THE AUTHOR

Anne Ake edited an arts magazine for eight years and owned and published *Cool KidStuff,* a children's magazine, with her daughter. She has published books and articles on many topics ranging from the arts to nature. She currently edits and designs a newsletter for the state parks in the northwestern region of Florida. As a freelance computer-graphic and desktop-publishing specialist, Ake designs brochure and page layouts, and as marketing manager of the Quality of Life Division of a navy base, Ake publicizes base leisure and recreational facilities and activities.